LOCK, STOCK & BARREL

LOCK, STOCK

&

BARREL

**First published in Great Britain in 1998 by
PAST TIMES® Oxford, England**

Copyright © 1998 Complete Editions
Reprinted 1999

Typeset by David Onyett, Publishing & Production Services,
Cheltenham
Printed and bound in Great Britain for Imago

PAST TIMES®

INTRODUCTION

Every day we make use of hundreds of words and phrases without giving a thought to what they really mean or how they entered the language – and there is no reason why we should.

Language is alive, growing and ever-changing. New words and phrases are introduced into everyday usage, reflecting the lives we lead and the world about us, while others fade away to take up retirement in dictionaries of language history. We use language to convey our feelings and ideas, our thoughts and our wishes. Language changes as we change and down the centuries the English language has grown to be one of the richest and most expressive the world has ever known.

Lock, Stock & Barrel represents a selection of familiar words and sayings: the ones that have the most interesting histories and frequently unexpected origins, many of which shed fascinating light on the daily lives of our forebears. We find words like 'freelance' and 'henchman', and phrases like 'pinning your heart on your sleeve', that have come down to us directly from the days of medieval warfare and chivalry. Britain's maritime heritage has brought ashore many expressions which once had specific meanings aboard ship, but have now cast adrift their nautical roots to enjoy a far wider general use. Riding and travel by coach may have been superseded by later modes of transport, but their legacy is kept alive in expressions like 'post haste' and even 'cab', the popular word for a taxi.

English has also benefited from the influence of many other languages. Throughout the book there are references to the old Nordic languages brought to these shores by the waves of settlers who arrived from Scandinavia and northern Europe in the centuries before the Norman Conquest. French, of course, the language of the new Norman rulers, introduced many words and expressions that still echo in English today. In later centuries colonies and former colonies of the British Empire were the seed-bed for fresh arrivals like 'barbecue', 'climbing on the bandwagon', 'doolally', 'mufti' and 'OK'. Then there are those individuals, long since forgotten by history, but who planted themselves in the language for some memorable action and whose names are kept alive in expressions like 'bold as brass', 'boycott', 'codswallop', 'Hobson's choice', and 'Namby-pamby'.

With a language as diverse and extensive as English, only a tiny portion can be analysed here. However, the backgrounds and 'biographies' included in *Lock, Stock & Barrel* reveal the secrets behind many of the words and expressions we use and hopefully may inspire further investigation of what lies hidden behind others.

Above board

To be 'above board' is to be honest and open to view; the opposite is to be secretive, hidden from sight and by association fraudulent. The term comes from the card table (the board) at which cheats would drop their hands below the table, in order to change their cards to form a more favourable hand. When all play is 'above board' there can be no suspicion of trickery.

Achilles heel

In ancient Greek mythology Achilles was dipped into the River Styx by his mother Thetis, to make him invulnerable. In doing this Thetis held her young son by one heel and, although she totally immersed him, this heel remained untouched by the water. As a result the great Greek hero of the Trojan wars grew to manhood with one weak spot, the heel his mother had held. It was an arrow wound in this heel that finally slew him and an 'Achilles heel' has been a weak spot ever since.

Acid test

The 'acid test' is the process that proves something beyond doubt and the expression comes from the test used to confirm whether or not a metal is gold. For gold is not effected by the majority of acids. The one that it is certain to react with is a mixture of concentrated nitric and hydrochloric acid. In medieval alchemy this was given the Latin name Aqua Regia, meaning 'royal water', because it dissolved the king of metals.

Adam's apple

The Biblical story of Adam consuming the forbidden fruit in the Garden of Eden was used as an explanation for the characteristic bulge in the larynx found in male throats. According to this account a piece of the apple given to Adam by Eve stuck in his throat and has shaped male throats ever since.

Agog

To be 'agog' is to be in a state of eager anticipation of a forthcoming development and draws its inspiration from the Old French expression *en gogues* which meant 'mirthful'.

All at sixes and sevens

One of several expressions describing a state of confusion, or an inability to reach an agreement, this has a curious ancestry. While it may be associated with the throwing of dice, there is tradition based on historical events that links it to a dispute that took place towards the end of the fifteenth century between two of the livery companies in the City of London. The Merchant Taylors and the Skinners received their charters within a few days of each other early in the fourteenth century. However, they failed to agree which company should be sixth and which seventh in the order of companies as they processed through the city. The matter was resolved by agreeing that they would take it in turns, with one company occupying sixth place one year and the other occupying it the following year. Once this had been resolved it could be said that they at least were no longer 'at sixes and sevens'.

All my eye and Betty Martin

This strange expression, which now means that something is all nonsense, has an uncertain origin. Traditionally it is thought to be the garbled version among British sailors of the prayer of request heard abroad, 'O mihi, beate Martine', which means 'Oh grant me, blessed St Martin'. 'It's all my eye...' is an older saying.

All ship-shape and Bristol fashion

In the days of sail when Bristol was one of the largest ports in England, it had a reputation for efficiency. That has been passed down in this popular turn of phrase which describes being totally prepared and ready for an undertaking, just as a well-organized ship would be prior to setting out on a voyage.

Apple of his eye

In Biblical times the pupil was thought to be a round solid ball like an apple, sitting in the centre of the eye. From that, its figurative meaning developed to cover anything deemed to be precious and worthy of careful protection.

Apple-pie order

For something to be in apple-pie order everything needs to be perfectly arranged in its proper place, neat and in order. Cooking, delicious as the outcome may be, has nothing to do with this. Its origins most likely lie in two Old French expressions: *cap à pied*, which came from medieval warfare and meant fully armed from 'head to foot'; and *nappes pliées*, the French for 'folded linen', bringing ideas of neatly folded, crisply ironed sheets and other linen.

At loggerheads

People 'at loggerheads' with each other are in a state of disagreement. A 'logger' is the name given to the heavy wooden block once used to hobble horses to prevent them from straying. As an extension of this a 'loggerhead' equates to a 'blockhead' and perhaps to be 'at loggerheads' with someone was seen by others as being locked in a state in which neither would give way and both parties were mindlessly obstinate.

At the end of one's tether

A tethered animal can graze as far as its rope, or 'tether', will allow it to move from the point at which it is 'tethered'. The image here is of the animal arriving at the full extent of the 'tether' and unable to move further. Fettered in this way, the animal might be expected to feel intensely frustrated and this is the sense in which the phrase is used with regard to people whose patience and self-control has been exhausted to the point of total despair or utter frustration.

Augury

In ancient Rome a favourable augury was taken as a sign that the gods approved a proposed course of action. The Roman 'augurs' were religious officials whose duty it was to interpret the *auspices* to decide on the attitudes of the gods.

    [See: auspices]

Auspices

Two Latin words *avis* (a bird) and *specere* (to observe) are combined to produce 'auspices'. In ancient Rome an *auspex* was a priest charged with observing the flight of birds to interpret the omens of a future enterprise. If the omen was favourable the enterprise would take place 'under the auspices' of the initiator of the plan.

An axe to grind

Anyone with an axe to grind offers help or friendship with an eye to furthering some personal interest or advantage. As a boy, the American statesman Benjamin Franklin had first-hand experience of someone with 'an axe to grind'. Persuaded by flattery, the young Franklin turned the heavy grindstone while the owner of the axe sharpened his blade. When the job was finished the man with the axe laughed at Franklin for his foolishness. For the rest of his life Franklin was suspicious that those who flattered him might merely be others 'with an axe to grind.'

Back to Square One

In the days when football matches were first broadcast, radio programmes printed pitch diagrams divided into numbered squares. Commentators referred to these squares to help listeners follow the course of the game. To go 'back to Square One' is to return to where one started.

Baker's dozen

A 'baker's dozen' contains thirteen items as opposed to the familiar twelve. This dates from the time when bakers were subject to heavy fines if they served under-weight bread. To avoid this danger bakers provided a surplus number of loaves, the thirteenth loaf in the dozen being called the vantage loaf.

Bald as a coot

The common coot is a bird with a white bill and front shield, which make it look bald. To be as 'bald as a coot' then, is to be totally bald.

Bank holidays

Before there were official public holidays there were bank holidays. Until 1830 the Bank of England was officially closed for more than forty days in the year. This number was reduced to eighteen and by 1834 it dropped to just four. With some minor amendments they have remained more or less the same ever since and the official bank holidays became adopted as general public holidays.

Barbecue

The English word 'barbecue' owes its origins to a Spanish word *barbacoa* which was current in the West Indies as a description for a wooden framework built on posts. From this idea a 'barbecue' became a wooden bedstead and also a similarly shaped framework made of iron on which a large animal could be roasted. From the cooking device, 'barbecue' had only to make a short step to the outdoor party at which the food is cooked and eaten.

Bare-faced

Today 'bare-faced' is used to describe those whose behaviour is impudent and brazen. In its original meaning 'bare-faced' had a more wholesome ring, implying openness and honesty, for a 'bare face' was a beardless face, where everything was plain to see and nothing could be concealed.

Barking up the wrong tree

This descriptive turn of phrase implying wasted or misdirected effort derives from the North American method of hunting racoons. Traditionally racoons were hunted in the dark and dogs were used to identify the trees up which racoons had escaped. It was not uncommon for dogs to be mistaken in the dark, barking up the wrong tree when the racoon had found refuge elsewhere.

Barmy

To be 'barmy' covers varying degrees of mental derangement from mild dottiness to total insanity. As a yeast, 'barm' produces a froth, leading to associations of empty-headedness.

Barracking

Most people know what 'barracking' is when they hear it, but explaining how the word came into being isn't as easy. One thing that is certain is that 'barracking' first came into regular usage in Australia towards the end of the nineteenth century as an expression that summed up the noisy jeering by spectators at things that displeased them at football and cricket matches. There is an Australian aboriginal word *borak* which means 'fun' or 'chaffing', which may have been combined with the Cockney word *barrakin* meaning 'a jumble of words'. The origin of 'barracking' may lie in the alliance of these two. However, there is an equally valid geographical explanation associated with football games played close to the Victoria Barracks in Melbourne. The rough crowds that came to watch these games were known as 'barrackers'.

Bean feast

Today's annual outing or special occasion, dates from an earlier feast given once a year by an employer for his or her employees. At many bean feasts held at the end of the year, a bean goose was commonly served. This large grey bird arrives in England in the autumn and gets its name from the bean-shaped mark on its bill. Beans themselves were frequently served as an important addition to the 'bean feast'.

Bear up

When things aren't going well, 'bearing up' is a determined gesture to keep one's spirits up with an outward display of self-confidence. It probably derives from the piece of harness sometimes used on carriage horses to hold their heads high. This was called a 'bearing rein' and prevented the horses from dropping their heads from a proudly arched position.

Bearing the palm

To 'bear the palm' is to be the best, because in ancient Rome it was customary for victorious gladiators to be given a branch from a palm-tree as a symbol of their success.

Beat about the bush

This is another term that comes from the sporting field. To 'beat about the bush' is to tackle a subject in a cautious, roundabout way, as opposed to adopting a direct, headlong approach. This mirrors the careful way in which sportsmen might beat a bush to flush out any game that are hiding in the thicket.

Beefeaters

The Yeoman Warders of the Tower of London have been referred to as 'beefeaters' since the middle of the seventeenth century. The name distinguishes them as servants of higher rank than 'loafeaters', since 'eater' was a term once used to describe a servant. Self-evidently, 'beefeaters' enjoyed a higher standard of living than 'loafeaters'.

Before you can say Jack Robinson

There are two likely candidates for the identity of the original Jack Robinson. The first was the late eighteenth-century English politician, John Robinson, who was accused of bribery on the floor of the House of Commons. When his accuser, the playwright and MP Richard Brinsley Sheridan, was asked to name the member of the government under suspicion, he looked directly across at Robinson and replied, 'I could name him as soon as I could say Jack Robinson'. The second was the central character in Thomas Hudson's popular composition *Jack Robinson* which appeared at the beginning of the nineteenth century. Returning home to find his beloved married to another, he went back to the sea 'afore you could say Jack Robinson'. Either way, 'before you can say Jack Robinson' has been passed down over nearly two centuries as another way of saying 'immediately', 'in an instant'.

Below the belt

According the Queensberry Rules it is prohibited in a boxing match for a competitor to strike an opponent below the waistband. So to hit 'below the belt' is to behave in an unfair and possibly cowardly fashion.

Bench-mark

In the days before modern surveying equipment, bench-marks were of greater significance than nowadays. The 'bench-mark' comprised a broad arrow shape, pointing upwards, topped by a horizontal line. This was carved by surveyors into a fixed location such as the side of the building or a rock-face. Here it acted as a starting point for measuring altitudes in the surrounding area. When a surveyor set about his work, an angle-iron was fixed in the horizontal cut to create the 'bench' on which the levelling-staff could be fitted. In this way a bench-mark has entered the language as a fixed point, from which further work can be undertaken.

Betwixt wind and water

To a sailor the point on a ship's hull that is 'betwixt wind and water' is the point about the waterline that is sometimes below water, sometimes above it, depending on the weather and sea conditions. To be holed 'betwixt wind and water' is to be placed in great danger of sinking. Hence the wider use of the expression to describe a situation of grave peril.

Beyond the pale

A 'pale' is a pointed stake used in a fence and by extension came to refer to the fence itself. In this way its meaning broadened to encompass the territory that lay within the boundary. This applied particularly to those areas of Ireland that were effectively under the control of the English crown during the Middle Ages. These shrank over the centuries and as they did so the areas 'beyond the pale' were regarded as returning to a wild and barbarous state. This meaning has survived as a description of someone's conduct that is outside the norms of civilized behaviour.

Bigwig

In the seventeenth and eighteenth centuries men of distinction wore large wigs as a mark of their exalted status. There are 'bigwigs' today in positions of importance in the law, where the Lord Chancellor and judges still wear full wigs. 'Bigwigs', as referred to in this expression, are people of importance in any capacity.

Birthday suit

Although the current understanding of 'birthday suit' is complete nakedness, the state in which we are born, there was a time when royal courtiers were expected to array themselves in specially commissioned suits of clothes to be worn on the sovereign's birthday.

Bistro

The 'bistro' is so quintessentially French that it comes as a surprise to discover that its origins probably lie in Russian. After the defeat of Napoleon at the Battle of Waterloo in 1815, Russian troops, among others, occupied Paris. There they frequented the city's bars and cafés where cries of *Bweestra* ('Quickly') soon became heard as the Russian soldiery demanded prompt service.

Bitter end

Today enduring hardship to the 'bitter end' brings with it resonances of stoic forbearance, suffered to the final blow of misfortune. This meaning may well come from a verse in the *Book of Proverbs*, 'But her end is bitter as wormwood'. However, the idea of something being taken to the very last extremity comes from the language of the sea where the 'bitts' were solid bollards made of wood or iron fixed to the deck, over which anchor cables were secured. In this way the 'bitter end' was the section of cable that always remained on board, even when the ship was lying at anchor.

Black-balled

To be black-balled is to be rejected, or refused admission to a club or similar institution. The term came about from the process used by existing members to vote on the eligibility of prospective candidates. Those in favour of a candidate dropped a white ball into a voting box or other container. Those against his election dropped in a black ball. In some instances the presence of just one black ball was enough to refuse entry to a new member, who could then consider himself 'blackballed'.

Black sheep

Black sheep were regarded as less valuable than white sheep and to the superstitious in by-gone days they were seen to be carrying the mark of the devil. From this developed the idea of the 'black sheep' as being a disgrace to his or her family or close community.

Blarney

The gift of the 'Blarney' is the power to talk one's way out of trouble, either to buy time or deceive an adversary. The word derives its meaning from an episode in Irish history when Cormac Macarthy employed the tactics of mild persuasive diplomacy to such effect, when his garrison was besieged in Blarney Castle early in the seventeenth century, that he talked his way out of the siege which failed as a result of his delaying tactics.

Blighty

During the First World War 'Blighty' was the soldiers' name for home, whether it be in Great Britain or some other part of the empire. But 'blighty' was first adopted many years before by British troops serving in India, who coined the phrase from the Hindi word *bilayati* meaning 'far away'.

Blowing hot and cold

The idea of an inconsistent person 'blowing hot and cold' as a result of being unable to decide what to do, comes from an ancient legend of a man given shelter and hospitality by a satyr. First the man blew on his fingers to warm them and almost in the same breath blew on the hot soup the satyr had given him in order to cool that. Irritated by his inability to make up his mind, the satyr packed him outside and sent him on his way.

Blue-stocking

Any woman of intellectual accomplishment runs the risk of being branded a 'blue-stocking', especially if she is seen to pay greater attention to her intellectual interests than to pandering to male ideals of what makes a woman attractive. The original 'blue-stockings' were members of an intellectual group formed in Venice at the beginning of the fifteenth century. Both men and women belonged to it and they distinguished themselves by wearing blue stockings as a mark of membership. The same use of blue stockings was taken up two centuries later by a group of women intellectuals in Paris and in the middle of the eighteenth century this society was copied in London under the name Bluestocking.

Bob's your uncle

As an expression of reassurance that things will turn out to your benefit, 'Bob's your uncle' owes its origins to a real life 'Bob', the Conservative Prime Minister Lord Salisbury, whose first name was Robert. During his administration in the late 1880s, his nephew A. J. Balfour was rapidly promoted through the cabinet until he was made Secretary of State for Ireland. Few could deny that Uncle Bob had served his nephew well.

Bold as brass

In 1770 it was still against the law to publish any account of the proceedings of Parliament and when the printer of the *London Evening News* broke the law he was sent before the chief magistrate for punishment. At that time the magistrate was Brass Crosby. He found in favour of the printer and released him, whereupon Brass Crosby was himself sent to the Tower. However, his imprisonment was short-lived after the people of London clamoured for his release and he was set free. His impudent stand against authority won him a place in the English language and many who have followed his example have been described as being 'as bold as Brass'.

Booby prize

The player who comes last in whist drives is known as the 'booby' and from this comes the tradition of awarding a small 'booby prize', frequently funny and always worthless, to the player or competitor who comes last in a competition.

Born in the purple

According to ancient custom Byzantine emperors ensured that their successors were born in a special room decorated in the imperial purple that signified their royal status. Since those times 'born in the purple' has come to be a metaphor for anyone born into a noble family.

Born with a silver spoon in your mouth

In days gone by it was traditional for godparents to present godchildren with silver spoons as christening presents. However, children born into well-to-do homes did not have to wait for their godparents to present them with their first taste of riches. Wealth was theirs at birth as they brought the 'silver spoon' with them into the world.

Boss your shot

In archery the 'boss' is the straw-filled base onto which the target is fixed. Anyone whose arrow missed the target completely and stuck in the boss was mocked by more accurate archers for his poor aim and was termed 'boss-eyed'. As a consequence to 'boss your shot' is to miss your aim completely. From the mid-nineteenth century 'boss-eyed' developed as a slang description of someone with an injured or defective eye.

Box and Cox

Box and Cox was the title of a nineteenth-century farce which tells the story of two men, Box and Cox, who are let the same room by their deceitful landlady. One occupant works all day, the other works all night and each makes use of the room wholly unaware of the other. From their predicament comes the expression to 'box and cox', meaning to alternate two or more situations simultaneously, frequently in a precarious manner.

Boycott

The phrase 'to boycott' an individual, an institution or a whole nation, is so widespread that it's surprising to discover that the term was only coined a century ago. The object of the first 'boycott' was a land agent in Ireland by the name of Captain Boycott. As an unpopular servant of an absentee landlord he was shunned by the local community who refused to have any social or business contact with him. They were following the political guidance of the Irish Land League which encouraged Irish peasants to treat anyone like Boycott as if he were 'a leper of old'.

A brace of shakes

'A brace of shakes' is a very rapid movement, the shaking twice of a dice-box, so it has come to express a sense of almost instantaneous action, or something accomplished very quickly. 'In a couple of shakes' or 'in two shakes of a lamb's tail' are similar examples.

Brand-new

Today 'brand-new' applies to anything that is very recently made and still untarnished from use. In its original meaning it applied solely to metals or objects made from metal and in this lies the root of the expression. In Old English a *brand* is a torch and, by extension, fire. So 'brand-new' meant fresh from the fire of the forge, from which metals emerged glowing and bright.

Bridegroom

The present-day word 'bridegroom' has developed from a confusion over two earlier words. In Old English the word for the man marrying the bride was *brydguma* meaning 'bride man'. However, the *guma* part of the word (meaning 'man') became confused over the centuries with the Middle English word *groom* for a 'man-servant'. This led to the replacement of *guma* with *groom* and the creation of 'bridegroom' as we know it today.

Bringing a question on the carpet

This expression which means, to raise a topic for discussion, reflects an earlier use of carpets as coverings for tables, before they were used exclusively on floors. A question brought 'on the carpet' was one laid before an assembly for discussion and debate.

Bring to book

When anyone is 'brought to book' they are asked to explain themselves, usually after some misdemeanour. In this case the 'book' refers to a written record or a code of practice which has or has not been followed by the person 'brought to book'.

Broaching a subject

Starting a conversation on a particular topic is frequently referred to as 'broaching a subject' and it draws its meaning from the process of drawing beer from a wooden barrel. In order to gain access to the beer, the barrel was tapped using a peg known as a *broach*. Once in place, the barrel could be opened and the beer started flowing.

Browned off

To be 'browned off' is to be bored and fed up, usually with the monotony of one's existence. In this context a 'brown' was slang for a penny and to be 'browned off' was to be given a penny to go away and leave the donor to get on with their own business. In addition to tedium, it carries with it echoes of rejection.

Bubble and squeak

This dish made from cold boiled potatoes and green vegetables fried together is named after the noises supposedly made during the cooking process. While they are boiled the ingredients *bubble* and once in the frying pan they *squeak* as they fry.

Buckshee

As a noun 'buckshee' meant extra rations. As an adjective it acquired the sense of something acquired for free or as a bonus.

The word was coined by British soldiers serving in India in the nineteenth century and was adapted from the Persian word *baksheesh*, meaning 'a tip' or 'a gratuity'.

Budget

British Chancellors of the Exchequer may have become familiar in the public eye for taking their budget statements to Parliament in a red case, but the association between the document and what it's carried in is closer than might first appear. In earlier times the documents detailing government income and expenditure were carried in a leather bag. An early French word for such a document wallet is *bougette*. In time the bag lent its name to its contents and Chancellors have been delivering 'budgets' ever since.

Bulling the barrel

When a wooden rum cask was nearly empty it was customary to pour in water to prevent the cask drying out and starting to leak. The mixture inside the barrel was nicknamed 'bull' among sailors who used the same expression when they made a second brew of tea, known as 'bulling the teapot'.

Burke a question

When a question, or any other statement is said to be 'burked', it is silenced, or stifled, as soon as it is raised. The phrase is derived from the surname of William Burke who, with his accomplice William Hare, suffocated victims and sold their bodies for medical research. Burke was hanged for his crimes in 1829 but his reputation lives on in this expression.

Burying the hatchet

By 'burying the hatchet' former adversaries agree to let bygones be bygones and bring their disputes to an end, so that they can start afresh. The phrase is said to recall the American Indian practice of symbolically burying hatchets and other weapons of war to mark the end of a conflict and the start of a mutually observed peace.

By and large

To understand something by and large, or to speak by and large, implies that one is approaching the subject in general terms rather than with detailed knowledge or experience. This is a term that dates from the days of sailing ships when to sail 'by' the wind described sailing very close to the wind and to sail 'large' was to sail with the wind on the quarter. Therefore a ship's overall ability to sail under different conditions was assessed by her ability to sail 'by and large'. As far as a helmsman was concerned, sailing 'by and large' meant sailing slightly off the wind, so that he had greater control of the ship and she was less likely to be 'taken aback' by a sudden change of wind direction.

[See: taken aback]

By hook or by crook

In the Middle Ages villagers were granted the right to gather firewood from their landlord's woods on the understanding that they only cut timber from trees which could be reached by a shepherd's crook and cut down with a bill-hook. That original meaning has been replaced by a sense of absolute necessity that one way or another a task will be accomplished or an objective reached. It is interesting to note that whereas the original meaning implied that this was a lawful activity, 'by hook or by crook' today implies that almost any means, right or wrong, will be employed to do what is necessary.

By the book

Once again 'the book' in this common expression is a notional work of authority, universally regarded as accurate and definitive on a given subject. To speak or behave 'by the book' is to follow precisely what is laid down as the accepted pattern without deviation.

By-the-by

Two uses of 'by' in this popular expression have two different meanings. The first 'by' has the same meaning as the French expression *en passant*: a sense of moving from one subject to the next. The second 'by' makes use of the meaning applied to words like 'by-road' and 'by-way', which are secondary thoroughfares stemming from main roads. 'By-the-by', therefore, means a secondary theme leading from the earlier or principal topic under discussion.

By the skin of my teeth

Teeth have no skin, of course. So to escape 'by the skin of one's teeth' is to get away by the narrowest margin. For the origin of this we have only to look to the Bible, where the phrase is used in the book of *Job*.

Cabinet

Although the Cabinet Room now used by the members of the British Cabinet is a room of ample proportions, the word Cabinet comes from an Italian word *cabinetto*, meaning a small room. It was in such intimate and secretive surroundings that the inner circle of government officers first met. Gradually the group meeting there became known by the name of the place where they met, much as the 'budget' took its name from the bag in which the financial documents were originally carried.

[See: budget]

Cabs

As an alternative name for a taxi, the English 'cab' is named after the french *cabriolet*, a light one-horse carriage which first appeared in London in the early nineteenth century. The French word stems from an Italian one, *capriola*, which describes the light-footed leaping of a goat. For, compared with the heavy lumbering coaches previously in use, the new cab was nimble and swift.

Caddie

These days the word 'caddie' is almost exclusively used to describe the person who carries a golfer's clubs around the course, or the little cart pushed by the golfer that has taken over from the caddie for the majority of golfers. In Scotland the word was a local form of 'cadet' and was previously used to describe errand boys and other men who earned their living in the streets.

Cadging

In former times pedlars carried their wares in a basket known as a 'cadge'. Since many of them no doubt begged or scrounged additional sustenance from the places they visited, their basket became synonymous with the act of begging or borrowing itself.

Calculate

This is such a familiar word that its origin, in the Latin word *calculi* (meaning 'pebbles) comes as quite a surprise. The Romans used small balls called *calculi* in their board abacuses on which they performed their mathematical calculations. Only when the results had been worked out were they written down in Roman numerals. Thus the process of using the pebbles to find the answer developed into the process we know as 'calculation'.

Called to the bar

The 'bar' which refers collectively to all professional barristers takes its name from the Inns of Court. There fully qualified barristers, or benchers, are separated from the students sitting in the main body of the hall by a partition, the 'bar'. When students have qualified as barristers, they are 'called to the bar' to be admitted as benchers.

Canopy

The English word 'canopy' has developed from the Greek word meaning 'gnat curtain'. This was the name given to the primitive mosquito nets used by fishermen on the River Nile, who used to raise their fishing nets on a pole before going to sleep beneath them. They did this in the knowledge that gnats will not fly through the mesh of a net. From this humble beginning grew the decorative hanging that now graces elaborate beds and pavilions, even royal thrones.

Canteen

The original meaning of 'canteen' was a wine cellar and all its subsequent meanings connected with sustenance and provisioning arise from this. So a 'canteen' became the place where food and drink were served. It also developed as the bottle of wine or water carried by soldiers. Even the cutlery canteen, shares this common origin. In this case the connection is with the canteen as a container.

Canter

The easy gallop on horseback familiar to riders is said to have been the pace preferred by medieval pilgrims riding towards Canterbury. The 'Canterbury gallop' or 'Canterbury trot' was shortened to 'canter' and as such entered the language of riding in the eighteenth century.

Carat

Precious stones are weighed in 'carats' and the purity of gold is judged in 'carats'. The word probably comes from the Arabic *qirat* meaning 'the seed of the locust tree' which was used for weighing gold and precious stones.

Carrying too much canvas

When a sailing ship hoisted more sail than she could safely carry in the wind, she was said to be 'carrying too much canvas'. The phrase has passed into general usage to describe the act of undertaking something that far exceeds the resources available to fund it.

Carrying weight

An argument or a person 'carrying weight' is one that has influence. But the term derives from horse-racing, in which the weights between riders is equalized by weight being added to the lighter ones.

Carte blanche

These two French words literally mean a blank paper. As such it was a document used in an unconditional military surrender on which the defeated commander merely signed his name, leaving the victors to fill in their own terms and conditions. From this has grown its broader figurative meaning allowing complete freedom of action to someone given 'carte blanche'.

Casting vote

A casting vote is the vote of the chairman of a meeting which is used to resolve an issue when the other votes are equal. In these circumstances the chairman's vote turns or 'casts' the final outcome.

Catch as catch can

In the form of wrestling of the same name the wrestlers are allowed to grip their opponents in anyway and by any part of the body they can. Hence the meaning of getting all you can by whatever means.

[See: by hook or crook]

Catch crop

A catch crop is a quick-growing crop planted between the rows of a slower-growing main crop to increase productivity. Sometimes a catch crop is planted to make up for a crop that has failed.

Cat's paw

To be made a 'cat's paw' by someone else is to be tricked by them into doing something they prefer not to do themselves. The reference comes from a fable about a monkey who persuades his friend the cat to use his paw to pull chestnuts out of a fire for the monkey to eat.

Caucus

Prior to American elections politicians in all political parties meet to discuss the relative claims and merits of candidates. The term coined for this type of consultative gathering is a 'caucus', an American Indian word for an 'adviser'.

Chap

These days a 'chap' can be a man of any description, but when the expression was first coined it meant a merchant or trader. This came about through the word 'chapman' which developed from the Old English word for a trader *ceapman*. Thus a good 'chapman', became a good 'chap', who in turn lost his particular line of business and became a good 'fellow'.

Charlatan

As a quack or an impostor a 'charlatan' is the anglicized form of the Italian word *ciarlatano* meaning a 'swindler' or a 'quack'.

Charley Moore

Anything described as being 'Charley Moore' was, in naval slang, honest, upright and respectable. This unusual mark of distinction is said to have originated in Malta where a publican in the middle of the nineteenth century advertised his premises with a sign that read 'Charley Moore – the Fair thing'. In contrast anything that was not 'Charley Moore' was deemed to be underhand and dishonest.

Charm

Although a 'charm' is generally thought of as an object that brings good luck or wards off evil, the word originally meant the incantation or spoken spell that was used to achieve the same protection. This is closer to the word from which 'charm' originated. That is the Latin word *carmen* meaning a song or verse.

Chatterbox

Chatterboxes existed before the name was applied to talkative people. There are references to 'chatter-baskets', people whose non-stop flow of talk was likened to the sound of a child's rattle. A similar noise was attributed to the dish rattled by beggars to collect alms. These were called 'clack-dishes' in Shakespeare's day.

Checkmate

'Checkmate' is the term used in chess when an opponent's king is placed in a position of check from which it cannot escape. The expression, like the game itself, comes from the Middle East and echoes two Arabic words *shah mat* which mean 'the king is helpless'.

Chestnut

As a tired old joke, repeated so often it is known to most people, a 'chestnut' came into popular usage through an early nineteenth-century melodrama *The Broken Sword*. One of the characters in this constantly repeats the same jokes, with only minor variations. During the play he is telling another character, Pablo, a joke about a cork tree when Pablo interrupts him to say the tree was a chestnut. To emphasize the point he says he's been told the joke twenty-seven times and by now he's sure the tree is a chestnut.

Chintz

'Chintz' is an unusual word that has adopted a unique spelling and changed from a plural to a singular noun. When varicoloured cotton cloth with floral designs was first imported from the East in the seventeenth century it brought with it the Hindi word *chint* meaning 'variegated'. In time 'chint' became 'chints' as the cloth grew in popularity and with this the spelling was altered too until 'chintz' became accepted as the standard form of the word.

Chipping in

This has two meanings: to contribute towards something and to interrupt. In the first case 'chipping in' takes its meaning from the game of poker in which players place chips, representing their money, in the 'pot'. This may also be the source of the meaning in which 'chipping in' implies interrupting someone as they are speaking, to make a point of one's own.

Chock-a-block

When something is 'chock-a-block' it is filled right up with no space left. In naval terminology it describes the situation when two blocks used in a tackle are pulled together so that neither of them can be moved any further. In this context 'chock' means 'close up to' and when one block is so close to another that it cannot move it is 'chock-a-block'.

Chop-chop

Like many expressions now widely used in English, 'Chop-chop' entered the language by way of Pidgin English in which *chop* developed the meaning 'quick'. So 'Chop-chop' came to mean 'quick, quick' or 'get a move on'.

[See: Pidgin English]

Chops of the Channel

Used in this phrase, 'Chops' adopts the meaning 'jaws'. And the 'Chops of the Channel' is the old name given by sailors to the entrance into the English Channel from the Atlantic.

Chore

'Chore' is the American version of the English word 'chare' and both share the meaning of repetitive work, frequently housework. They derive this meaning from the Old English word *cerran* which means 'to turn'. From this comes the sense of work that requires regular attention.

Civil List

These days the Civil List refers to the annual grant made by Parliament to the Crown and the Royal Family, but when it first came into existence in the reign of William of Orange at the beginning of the eighteenth century, judges and Civil Servants also received their salaries from the same funds. Their association with it has long since ended but their original connections survive in the term Civil List.

Clap-trap

The first 'clap-trap' was used in the theatre as a means of winning applause at any price. So 'clap-trap' consisted of cheap stunts and jokes that were sure to go down well with the audience in the pits. Since then 'clap-trap' has widened its terms of reference to cover any sort of worthless nonsense.

Clear as a bell

The fact that the tone of a bell can be heard a considerable distance away gave rise to this expression. However, the sound that carries clearly to the ear has since been confused with unpolluted water, or other liquid, or a cloudless sky which are clear to the eye.

Clew up

On a sailing ship a 'clew' was the corner of the sail to which ropes were attached. When a sail was 'clewed up' the corners were hauled up to the yard from which it was suspended, so that the sail could be furled. From this has grown the meaning of 'clew up' to finish something completely, to be ready to do something with everything fully prepared.

Climbing on the bandwagon

In days gone by it was common in the USA for a band to be paraded on a wagon through the streets to advertise political meetings or other public gatherings. In the case of meetings held prior to elections, local dignitaries showed their support for candidates by climbing onto their particular wagons. Since then 'climbing on a bandwagon' has been taken as a display of support for a popular movement in the hope of personal profit or advantage.

Clinch

When an argument is 'clinched' or a business deal is 'clinched' they are reckoned to be firmly fixed once and for sure. The same expression is used by carpenters who 'clinch' the pointed ends of nails by bending them back on themselves to hold them fast. This sense of being fixed securely in many cases makes 'clinch' synonymous with 'clench'.

Clink

To be thrown in the clink today is to be sent to any prison. However, in the sixteenth and seventeenth centuries the 'Clink' was a specific prison in the London borough of Southwark which was in use until 1780, when it was destroyed by rioters.

Clue

'Clue' is another spelling of 'clew' (see above), one that picks up on an earlier meaning of 'clew', which is a 'ball of thread'. It was a ball of thread, or 'clue', like this which helped Theseus find his way out of Minator's labyrinth in the ancient Greek myth that tells his story. In the same way more familiar 'clues' today help us unravel puzzles and mysteries.

Cocking a snook

A 'snook' is a derisive gesture made by placing the thumb on the nose and spreading the fingers. 'Cocking a snook' lends to this an air of swaggering defiance, alluding to the stance of fighting cocks. The adjective 'cocky' follows a similar meaning.

Codswallop

'Codswallop' today is a disparaging way of dismissing ideas and opinions as stupid nonsense, especially when they are offered as serious information or instruction. When the word was coined a little over a century ago 'Codswallop' referred specifically to a newly invented soft drink. This was created by Hiram Codd, who developed a novel type of mineral water bottle which used a marble, held in the neck by the pressure of the gas inside the bottle, as a stopper. At that time *Wallop* was a slang word for beer. So 'Codd's Wallop' was the derogatory name given by beer drinkers to Mr Codd's mineral waters and similar soft drinks. Since then the word has acquired a broader, but no less disparaging meaning.

Come up to scratch

'Scratch' in this context has a sporting reference. Contests of various types, notably running races, began with competitors lining up along a mark literally scratched in the ground. A line like this was used in early boxing matches too. In this case the two contestants had to begin each round standing with one foot touching a line scratched in the ground. Any contestant who failed 'to come up to scratch' at the start of a round lost the contest.

Coming a cropper

'Coming a cropper' means falling badly, either physically or as a figure of speech. On a bird the 'crop' is the craw in its gullet and to fall on the craw or 'crop' meant falling so heavily that even this part of the neck hit the ground – hence 'coming a cropper'.

Copper-bottomed

The phrase 'copper-bottomed' brings with it a reassuring sense of security. For something to be 'copper-bottomed' it is reckoned to be less risky, a better bet in other words than whatever else is on offer. When the expression first came into use it referred specifically to ships that were 'copper-bottomed', that is those with hulls lined with copper. These were reckoned to be faster and more secure that purely wooden-hulled ships and consequently they presented a more attractive investment and a safer risk to insurers.

Cotton on

There may not appear to be an obvious connection between the early days of the textile industry and gaining an understanding of a line of thought, but to 'cotton on' is nevertheless derived from 'cotton' the fabric. By the fifteenth century 'cotton' was established as a verb meaning 'to provide a nap' or 'to take on a nap' which no doubt arose from the finishing process that produced a nap on cotton cloth. Two centuries later 'cotton' had acquired the meaning of 'to get on with' and by the nineteenth century it was being used in the sense of 'to take to'. Its present-day meaning of 'to catch on' to an idea or a way of thinking can be seen as an extension of these developments.

Creaking doors hang the longest

Frail and weak as someone may appear to be, he or she will often outlive those who seem fitter and more robust. These words of comfort were offered to the elderly or infirm. A less charitable interpretation may associate the aggravating noise of a creaking door with the constant demands sometimes made by the elderly and sick on those who look after them.

Criss-cross

The modern meaning of 'criss-cross', to cross from side to side, or a pattern made from crossing lines, developed from the medieval hornbook. This was a thin board covered with a sheet of transparent horn, beneath which was written the Lord's Prayer, the Roman numerals, an exorcism and the alphabet. At the beginning and end of the alphabet was a cross, similar in shape to a Maltese cross. In time this became known after the two crosses as a Christ-cross row, which was gradually shortened and modified to the 'criss-cross' we recognize and use today.

Cross-patch

In the sixteenth century a dolt or a fool was called a 'patch' and 'cross-patch' was a foul-tempered fool. Today the association with stupidity has largely disappeared but 'cross-patches' remain, especially among tired children.

Crying stinking fish

People who 'cry stinking fish' openly underestimate and decry their own achievements or abilities, just as the street sellers of days gone by used to 'cry' their wares as they walked about.

Cudgelling your brains

When you have to make an extreme and metaphorically painful effort to remember or understand something you are 'cudgelling your brains'. The idea comes from the old-fashioned school-room where pupils were beaten with a stick in the mistaken belief that this would improve their intelligence or further their understanding of their lessons.

Currying favour

At first acquaintance this is a strange expression but when one discovers that it arises from the stable rather than the kitchen, it begins to make sense. 'Currying' is a term used in riding circles for rubbing down or grooming a horse. In this expression it was not 'favour' that was first curried; it was 'favel', the fallow or chestnut horse. For some reason 'currying favel' was taken as a sign of deceitfulness in the Middle Ages. Since that time the expression has changed to 'currying favour', which makes greater sense in the context in which it is now used, that is to say trying to win the good opinion of others by excessive flattery.

Cut of his jib

This is another nautical expression adopted by landlubbers. The 'cut of the jib' (the foresail) on old-fashioned sailing vessels was taken by some as an indication of the nature of the ship and the way she handled. It was a snap judgement much as the assessment of a person's character by their appearance. So the 'cut of his jib' equates to 'the look of him'.

Cutting the painter

In this context a 'painter' is the light rope used to tie a small boat to a large craft or to moor it alongside a quay or jetty. 'Cutting the painter' meant setting the small boat free, an irrevocable act that would most likely result in its loss. So the phrase acquired a wider use for the severing of a long-standing connection.

Dab-hand

If a 'dab-hand' at something, an expert in other words, is also described as being 'adept', the origins of 'dab-hand' become clearer. The Latin word *adeptus* was used to describe someone who had reached a given standard in a craft or other profession. 'Dab' is a shortened form of the Latin word and 'dab-hand' recalls the manual origins of the phrase.

Dander

Asking someone if their 'dander is up' is to ask if they are excited and enraged. In the nineteenth century 'dander' was a substance used to ferment molasses, which helps to explain the origins of the expression, conveying the same idea of getting over-heated. However, there is a Dutch expression *op donderen* meaning 'to burst into rage', which uses the word *donderen* ('lightning') to describe the state someone is in when their 'dander is up'. Either way, the meaning is clear, though if you want to avoid a dusty answer, it's probably best not ask the question in the first place.

Darby and Joan

Darby and Joan have been the epitome of a truly faithful, old-fashioned couple since they first appeared together in print in a ballad by Henry Woodfall which was first published in 1735. In his youth Woodfall had been served as an apprentice to John Darby, who was a printer by trade.

Daylights

In the language of early fist-fighters 'daylights' was a slang expression for 'eyes'. So to 'darken his daylights' was to give someone a black eye and to 'beat the living daylights out of him' was to give him a thorough beating.

Dead as the Dodo

The poor old Dodo owes its unfortunate name to Portuguese sailors who first spotted it on the island of Mauritius and named it *doudo*, meaning 'silly'. The Dodo was a large flightless bird belonging to the pigeon family. Hunted to extinction by the end of the seventeenth century, it is remembered now in this expression used to describe something that is hopelessly out-of-date and long since dead and buried.

Dead as a door-nail

The 'door-nail' is the large, broad-headed metal stud on which the door-knocker strikes. Anything on the receiving end of such constant and unrelenting rapping is reckoned to be well and truly dead.

Deaf as a beetle

This has nothing to do with an insect that's hard of hearing. In this case the *beetle* in question is a heavy wooden mallet used to knock in posts, drive in wedges, or level paving slabs.

The Devil dances in an empty pocket

An empty pocket is a temptation to robbery. In days gone by many coins carried a cross on one side, so the Devil would never go into a pocket containing 'holy' coins. The only pockets he felt comfortable in were, of course, ones that were empty of coins.

The Devil to pay and no pitch hot

Here is another nautical expression with a specific meaning. The 'devil' was a seam on board wooden-hulled ships that was hard to get at and always required more pitch than any other when the gaps in the hull were being sealed to make it watertight. The expression has come down to us meaning that serious trouble is likely to arise as a result of whatever has happened.

Digs

The use of 'digs' to describe lodgings, usually of a temporary nature, first became current in the USA where the word started out in the longer form of 'diggings', the temporary accommodation of gold miners during the California gold rush. The word began to be used in the UK from the middle of the nineteenth century.

Ditto

'Ditto' means 'the same again'. Originally an Italian word, it is drawn from the Latin *dictum* meaning something that 'has been said'.

Donkey's years ago

This is an example of an expression that has altered its spelling over time. 'Not for donkey's ears' means not for a very long time and refers, of course, to the length of a donkey's ears. However, the *y* gradually stretched from the 'donkey' and turned 'ears' into 'years'. The meaning of the expression is the same, if it does make rather less sense than the original.

Don't look a gift horse in the mouth

Examining a horse's teeth is a popular method of gauging how old it is and this proverb advises those who receive gifts against trying to discover what they cost, or what they're worth. The advice is, be happy to have received the gift and leave it at that.
    [See: straight from the horse's mouth]

Doolally

Anyone said to have gone 'doolally' is behaving in a peculiar, unbalanced way. The word comes from India, where British troops who had completed their period of military service were sent to Deolali camp to await their voyage home. There long periods of boredom and the effects of the climate may have caused some to become deranged.

Double Dutch

In the days when the Dutch epitomized 'foreigners' in the eyes of the English, anyone speaking 'double Dutch' was reckoned to be talking in an even more incomprehensible way than a foreigner.

Drawing a blank

To draw a blank is to fail to achieve or find what one set out for. The phrase originated, not at the gaming table as might be expected, but in the sporting field, where likely coverts would be 'drawn' in the hope of flushing out game only to find that there was no game there.

Dyed in the wool

The opposite of superficial and short-lived, 'dyed in the wool' came into use in the textile industry. Cloth that was dyed before weaving, dyed in the wool in fact, kept its colour much better than that dyed after weaving – cloth 'dyed in the piece'.

Earmarked

An object that is 'earmarked' is one that has been set aside for a particular purpose. Earmarking in this context recalls the agricultural practice of marking the ears of stock, so that their ownership can be easily identified.

Eating humble pie

Anyone made to 'eat humble pie' is forced to come down from a lofty position they had previously adopted, in order to defer to others and frequently suffer humiliation at the hands of those they had formerly looked down on. This sense of hierarchy comes from the traditions of the medieval hunting feast in which a clear distinction was drawn between the food served to the lord and his peers, and the huntsmen of lower station. While the lord and household were served venison at their high table, the huntsmen and lower orders were seated further down the table where they were given the deer's entrails, or 'umbles', made into a pie. 'Humble pie' is a pun on this 'umble pie' and those served it are made to eat inferior food in an inferior position.

Eavesdropping

Listening furtively to other people's conversations, as conveyed by this unusual word, may seem a far cry from architecture, but that is where its origin lies. In the case of a building without gutters, the 'eavesdrop' was the narrow strip of ground around the outside of the walls where water dripped from the eaves. So anyone who wanted to listen to what was being said inside a building, had to stand 'within eavesdrop' in order to hear.

Even break

The 'even break' referred to here is an equal opportunity, a fair chance, in the coursing field. Here a pair of greyhounds were set loose in pursuit of a hare. To ensure fair competition, the two had to be set free of their leash at the same time, thus giving them an 'even break'.

Fag-end

The 'fag-end' is the very last bit of something, the piece that is left over when the more desirable pieces have gone. The term comes from the textile industry where the 'fag-end' of a piece of cloth was the end piece, often consisting of coarser material.

Fagged out

To be 'fagged out' is to be in a state of near total exhaustion, with no strength left. In this case 'fag' refers to a rope's end that has become untwisted and is thereby weaker than it was in its original state.

Falling foul of

Falling foul of someone is to get on bad terms with them as a result of words or action. The term comes from the language of the sea where a rope is 'foul' when it becomes entangled and where an anchor with its rope twisted round it is said to be 'fouled'. Ships can 'foul' each other too, when the passage of one impedes that of another vessel.

Falling on your feet

Unexpected good fortune, when a potential catastrophe turns to one's advantage, is often referred to as 'falling on your feet'. The image is drawn from the popular belief that cats invariably manage to land on their feet and therefore avoid serious injury even when falling from considerable heights. And cats, one should remember, are supposed to be blessed with nine lives.

Fans

There have been fanatic admirers throughout history, but 'fans' as we know them today were only referred to as such at the beginning of the twentieth century. The term 'fan' originated as a simple abbreviation of 'fanatic' and dates from the end of the seventeenth century.

Feather in your cap

Wearing a feather in one's cap was a sign of distinction, an honour recognized and observed in many parts of the world. In societies such as that of ancient Lycia (in what is western Turkey today) and among American Indians, each feather worn represented an enemy killed by the wearer.

Filthy lucre

'Lucre' owes its origins to the Latin word *lucrum* meaning 'gain', which in turn is linked to words in Greek and Sanskrit that apply to stolen goods. The Hindi word *lut* (pronounced the same way as the English word of the same meaning, 'loot') comes from a similar root. So lucre brings with it the taint of ill-gotten gains reinforced in the expression 'filthy lucre'.

Fine fettle

In Old English *fetel* meant 'bond' or 'girdle', from which has grown 'fettle' that develops this sense of binding, preparing, getting things in good order. So anything or anyone who is in 'fine fettle' is in good condition and ready for anything.

Fine words butter no parsnips

By tradition parsnips are usually garnished with butter before being served; without the butter, many would argue, the dish is incomplete, bland, even unpalatable. Hence the inference of this expression, that mere words alone achieve nothing.

Études
prises dans le bas Peuple
où
les Cris de Paris
premier Suitte
1737

Fitting to a 'T'

The allusion here is to a draughtsman's T-square, the ruler with a cross-piece at one end set precisely at right angles, which makes it possible to make accurate drawings, parallel lines and right angles. In this expression anything that 'fits to a T', fits exactly.

Flash in a pan

Any action that fails after a showy beginning can be described as a 'flash in a pan', because this was what happened in early flint-lock guns when gun-powder ignited in the lock-pan with a flash, but the main charge in the barrel did not. When this happened the gun failed to fire its charge.

Flogging a dead horse

This common expression evokes an image of effort uselessly expended on something that has no chance of continuation or success. However, it also refers back to a turn of phrase common among sailors in days gone by. In this context the 'dead horse' was work to be done but already paid for in advance. Aboard ship this usually amounted to the first month's wages at sea that were paid to the crew before they set sail. When the month was completed a symbolic 'dead horse' was dropped into the sea, to show that from then on every day worked on the voyage would be paid for.

Forking out

'Forking out' means paying over money, usually with some degree of reluctance. In this context 'fork' has nothing to do with a garden implement or even a piece of cutlery. Here it is used as a slang term for 'a finger'. So 'forking out' equates to 'handing over' what is due.

Freelance

Freelance workers in various professions have no permanent employment but offer their services to a variety of employers on a job-by-job basis. The original 'freelances' were literally that, medieval mercenaries who offered their fighting skills to the highest payer.

Frog in the throat

An unexpected and very brief loss of one's voice is jokingly referred to these days as having 'a frog in one's throat'. The image is humorous, if mildly repellent, but it dates from an age when people could theoretically get frogs in their throats from accidentally swallowing frog spawn in drinking water drawn from ponds and streams where it had been laid. According to folk tradition, tadpoles could hatch inside the unwitting drinker, in due course producing a fully developed frog. Should such a creature find its way back up the drinker's throat it might well cause a loss of voice.

From pillar to post

Anyone moving from pillar to post is in a constant state of flux, moving from one place to another, often with little purpose and frequently harassed as they go. This state of affairs has been linked to the ricocheting of tennis balls around the early walled enclosures where tennis was first played. There are also associations with punishment in the pillory followed immediately afterwards with a flogging at the whipping post.

Funnybone

The so-called 'funnybone' is a section of nerve in the human elbow that is close enough to the surface of the skin to be affected by knocks. The bone that lies above it is the humerus and in this lies the likely origin of the pun that has turned the 'humerus bone' into the 'funny bone'.

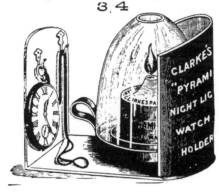

CLARKE'S
(REGISTERED)
**"PYRAMID" NIGHT LIGHT
WATCH HOLDER.**
With "Burglar's Horror" Lamp, and One
Box "Pyramid" Lights, complete in Box,
3 4

Gadget

'Gadgets' are generally small useful mechanical attachments that improve functions or make them easier to perform. Sailors were the first to refer to 'gadgets' although the term did not become widely adopted until mechanical devices produced as a result of the Industrial Revolution became part of everyday life. There is a French word *gachette* which describes a catch in a lock or the trigger mechanism in a gun, both typical of the earliest forms of 'gadgets'.

Gaga

We have the French language to thank for this less than charitable adjective sometimes applied to those who are showing signs of senile decay. 'Gaga' is not restricted to the elderly. Anyone considered to be half-witted can be described as 'gaga'. However, the French verb *gâter* means 'to impair' or 'to spoil' which may account for the association of its English descendant with declining faculties brought on by old age.

Game leg

A 'game' leg is a lame leg and understandably the expression has no associations with sport. It derives its meaning from a Celtic word *cam*, meaning 'bent', which is also the root of the French word of the same meaning *gambi*.

Getting down to brass tacks

In old-fashioned drapers' shops it was common for cloth to be measured against the shiny heads of brass tacks, driven into the counter at even distances apart. 'Getting down to brass tacks' recalls this process of determining precisely what was required.

Getting your ducks in a row

The image in this widely used American expression is one of organization and tidy thinking. Accurate as that may be, the image is not as straightforward as first appears. For in this instance 'ducks' are in fact skittles, not the more wayward farmyard fowls.

Gibberish

Although 'gibber' means to chatter incoherently, it entered the language later than 'gibberish' meaning unintelligible jargon or speech. 'Gibberish' may owe its origin to associations with 'Egyptian' (generally referring to Gypsy) speech and terminology. If that is the case, Romany, the language spoken by gypsies, would have been unintelligible to those uneducated in it.

Gift of the gab

Anyone possessing the 'gift of the gab' has a facility for fluent and frequently persuasive speech. The current turn of phrase dates from the eighteenth century, when *gab* meant 'talk'. A century earlier the expression was the 'gift of the gob' and 'gob' is still in use in slang as a word for 'mouth'.

Giving the mitten

From the end of the sixteenth century those who received a *mittimus* were dismissed from their posts. The word comes from the Latin verb *mittere* meaning 'to send'. 'Giving the mitten' is a nineteenth-century corruption of *mittimus* and was first used to mean jilting a sweetheart, in the sense of 'to send away'. It later acquired a broader meaning of simply 'to dismiss' which was closer to the earlier use of *mittimus*.

Going for a song

The 'song' that gave rise to this was a long poem called *The Faerie Queene* presented to Queen Elizabeth I by Edmund Spenser. In spite of the fact that this proved to be Spenser's most celebrated work, it failed to impress Lord Burleigh, the Lord High Treasurer. When he heard that the Queen proposed paying Spenser £100 for his work, his reply was reputedly 'What! All this for a song?' The money was eventually handed over at Queen Elizabeth's insistence, but the implication that it was paid for a mere trifle has lived on ever since.

Going haywrire

The wire used to bind bales of hay required careful handling to prevent it becoming entangled. The metaphor has been carried from the hay field and now anything that gets out of control can be said to have 'gone haywire'.

Going like one o'clock

This graphic expression dates from the times when the mid-day break in many work-places was the hour between one o'clock and two o'clock in the afternoon. As soon as the end-of-work signal was given at one o'clock workers streamed out to make the most of their free hour and the rate at which they left gave rise to this expression of eager haste.

Going off at half-cock

This is another metaphor from the days of early fire-arms and refers to a gun that goes off when the hammer is in the supposedly safe position of being half-cocked. With the hammer fully cocked the gun would be ready to fire, but a discharge when it was half-cocked would be a complete surprise and would probably result in a wasted shot. For anything else to go off 'at half-cock' means that it starts before one is ready and frequently results in failure and disappointment.

[See: hanging fire]

Going the whole hog

To 'go the whole hog' is to undertake an enterprise with the aim of seeing it through to completion without compromise or reservation. A 'hog' was slang for a 'shilling' and 'going the whole hog' meant spending the shilling all in one go. The phrase became a political catch-phrase in the USA during the 1828 presidential campaign when it was applied to Andrew Jackson, described as a 'whole-hogger' who would see a job through until it was finished without worrying about the consequences.

[See: lock, stock and barrel; the whole caboodle]

Gone for a Burton

This phrase became widely used during the Second World War as a euphemism for someone or something that had gone missing and was presumed lost for good. Various explanations have been put forward for its origins. Here are two of the most frequently given. The phrase gained considerable popularity in the RAF and it's possible that it came about from the training of radio operators which took place in the premises of Burton's the tailors in Blackpool. Those who failed were said to have 'gone for a Burton' and the term was soon applied to aircrew who went missing in action. Another common explanation is linked with a pre-war advertisement for Burton beer, which carried the catch-phrase 'Gone for a Burton' as an explanation for someone's absence.

Gone to pot

The modern equivalent of this commonly used phrase might well be 'past its sell-by date'. Both share a sense of something spoilt and no longer as acceptable as it once was. In its original sense 'gone to pot' referred literally to left-over meat that was only fit to be prepared as a rough stew of odds and ends and which was kept for this purpose in a special cooking pot.

[See: pot luck]

Good books

To be in someone's 'good books' is to be in favour with them and the expression comes from an earlier definition of a book which could amount to a single sheet of paper, or simply a list. In this context 'good books' amounted to a list of friends. In the same way 'bad books' was a list of adversaries.

Good wine needs no bush

The meaning of this somewhat obscure expression is that anything that has genuine merit or worth does not need to be advertised to the world at large. It stems from ancient Rome where it was customary for taverns to display an ivy bush to attract customers: ivy being sacred to Bacchus the god of wine.

Grasping the nettle

Touching a stinging nettle proves that if it is held tightly it is less likely to sting that if it is touched tentatively. This practical advice provides a metaphor for tackling difficulties resolutely rather than approaching them nervously.

Grass widow

When the term 'grass widow' was first used it described a woman who had had a child without first marrying the father. In this context 'grass' may have alluded to a bed of grass or hay, perhaps where the child was secretly conceived. That usage was current in the sixteenth century. Three hundred years later the phrase emerged in India in a more respectable context. Here it was used to describe women temporarily separated from their husbands, frequently because of unbearably hot weather which they escaped by moving to hill stations, while their husbands remained at their posts in the sweltering plains below.

Grog

Until the practice ceased in 1970, grog was the ration of rum diluted with water issued to ratings in the Royal Navy. Watered-down rum had first been introduced into the service 230 years earlier in place of the neat rum that was then being consumed by both officers and men. The man responsible for this was the then Commander-in-Chief West Indies, Admiral Vernon. He was nicknamed Old Grog by his men because of the grogram coat he wore, made of a coarse material spun from silk and wool. The name of the admiral was given to the drink he devised and the Navy has drunk 'grog' ever since.

Halcyon days

When 'halcyon days' were first spoken of they referred to a specific time of the year: the fourteen days either side of the winter solstice, the shortest day of the year. This was the period, according to ancient Sicilian folklore, in which the *halcyon*, the

Greek name for a 'kingfisher', laid its eggs on the surface of the sea and then incubated them. During this time it was believed that the surface of the sea remained calm and untroubled by waves. Those early 'halcyon days' have subsequently expanded to embrace any period of unruffled peace and contentment.

Hanging fire

Early guns which were slow to fire their charge after the gunpowder in the touch-hole had been lit were said to 'hang fire' and the expression has come to be used in any circumstances when there is a delay or when someone is slow to take action.

[See: going off at half-cock]

Hat-trick

Although 'hat-trick' is now used to describe success in various sports, the phrase originated in cricket where a bowler who took three wickets in successive deliveries was entitled to receive a new hat provided by his club. Hat-tricks are still notable feats in cricket and the term is also applied to a number of achievements repeated three times.

Having a dekko

'Having a dekko' is another example of an Indian word that was introduced into English by troops serving in India. It has been in common use since the end of the nineteenth century sharing its original meaning in Hindustani of having a 'look'.

Having a yen for

This turn of phrase first came into use in the USA where it described a strong desire for something. The *yen* in question is a Chinese word for opium smoke, which may account for the sense of craving in the expression.

Having no truck with

The old French word *troquer*, meaning 'to barter' is a pointer towards the background of this phrase. 'Having no truck with' someone is to avoid any dealings with them, especially to avoid any business dealings. At one time workers were paid all or part of their of their wages in accordance with the truck system, whereby they were paid in goods, or tokens that could be exchanged for goods, controlled by their employers. A series of government measures abolished the system during the nineteenth century by which time it had become totally discredited. 'Having no truck' in these circumstances meant a refusal to accept payment by the truck system.

Hear, hear!

This is a widely used way of expression approval for something a speaker has said. It dates from the time when disapproval was shown by humming. Those who were in favour of what was being said called for others to listen by saying 'Hear, him!'. Over time this changed to 'Hear, hear!', the form in which it is used today.

Henchman

The original meaning of 'henchman' was 'a man who attended to horses', in other words a groom or horseman. In German the word *hengst* means a 'stallion' and 'henchman' probably derives from a word formed from the same root combined with 'man'. From this earlier use 'henchman' has broadened in meaning and now applies to any solid supporter. Indeed it now brings with it unfavourable associations and these days 'henchmen' is frequently used to describe the supporters of dubious politicians and the leaders of criminal gangs.

Here's mud in your eye

This popular toast has a double-edge for, in proposing it, the speaker is actually asking those assembled to drink to his own good fortune. 'Here's mud in your eye' comes from the racing field where the ones receiving mud in their eyes would be behind the leading horse. The only rider in the race without mud in his eye would obviously be the one in front of the rest of the field.

Hiding your light under a bushel

People who are modest about their abilities are often said to 'hide their light under a bushel'. The 'bushel' was formerly a measure of dry goods, such as grain and the name was given to the container which measured each bushel. To be under a bushel, then, was to be hidden from sight.

High and dry

This is a reference to boats and ships left stranded by the retreating tide. To be left high and dry oneself is to be abandoned and excluded from the current of events.

Hob-nob

'Hob-nob' has a sense of 'give and take', the easy sharing that is part of friendship. This meaning becomes clearer when we understand that 'hob-nob' is a variant of 'hab-nab', meaning 'to have and not have'. In the eighteenth century 'hob-nob' meant drinking together. Since then it has acquired a wider meaning akin to 'share and share alike', which is an apt description of the close friendships in which we are happy to hob-nob with each other.

Hobson's choice

In reality 'Hobson's choice' amounts to having no choice at all. The phrase is said to take its name from a Cambridge horse-keeper and carrier by the name of Thomas Hobson, who insisted on only releasing his horses for use in the order stipulated by him. Those wishing to hire horses from him either accepted Hobson's choice or went without a horse.

Hoity-toity

Used as an adjective 'hoity-toity' describes those who are regarded by others as 'stuck-up'. However, 'hoit-toity' was also used as a noun and here it meant a 'frolic' or 'riotous behaviour', from the word 'hoit' meaning 'to indulge in a romp'. This may seem at odds with people who put on airs, but 'hoity-toity' has embraced both meanings, although it is as an adjective that we use it today.

Hoist with his own petard

In medieval warfare a petard was large metal container filled with gunpowder that was frequently raised alongside defences in order to destroy them when the petard was detonated. This was a risky business and it was not unknown for the engineers hoisting the petard into position to be killed by its premature detonation. Hence the expression we still use today to describe someone whose own strategy or device turns against him.

Holding the purse strings

At one time a purse consisted of a leather pouch drawn to a close with a string. Holding the purse strings ensured that you controlled when the purse was opened and therefore when money was spent or deposited in it. The design of purses may have changed over time, but the metaphor still holds true.

Honeymoon

According to ancient European custom, newly married couples used to drink a beverage made from diluted honey during the first month of their marriage and the sweetness of that first month together as man and wife has become firmly rooted in the language.

Hook line and sinker

The image in this expression is that of a fish that is enticed by a fisherman to swallow not only his baited hook, but the weight above it and some of the fishing line as well. The analogy in a wider context is that of a gullible listener who totally 'swallows' what has been said, no matter how implausible it might be.

The horns of a dilemma

To be in 'the horns of a dilemma' is to be faced by two equally unfavourable choices. The expression originates from the Greek word *lemma* meaning an 'assumption'. A *dilemma* is a double *lemma* which medieval philosophers perceived as being like a bull that would toss you, whichever horn you held.

Horse-play

Rough, knock-about entertainment is frequently referred to as 'horse-play', recalling the traditional antics of the hobby horse which was part of the company of folk dancers and performers who appeared as seasonal celebrations such as May-day and Christmas.

Hung on the nail

This expression dates from the era of the pawn shop and has survived as a euphemism for pawning something or pledging something of value in exchange for a loan. When goods were pawned, they were frequently hung on a numbered nail in the pawn-shop and the customer was given a duplicate number to be returned when the loan was repaid and the goods redeemed.

If the cap fits, wear it

Although fewer caps are worn now than in days gone by, this popular expression still survives. It means, if a remark is applicable to you, you should apply it to yourself. In the same way, many caps and hats look the same and may be the same size, but everyone knows his or her own cap or hat as soon as it is put on.

Ignoramus

Since the seventeenth century 'ignoramus' has been used as a noun describing someone so absolutely stupid that he or she knows nothing. Originally the word was a Latin legal term meaning 'we ignore it'. This was written on the back of indictments rejected by grand juries and refused admission to the courts.

In cahoots

This American expression meaning to be in partnership or in league with someone developed from the French word for a small hut, *cahute*. Presumably living with someone in confined surroundings required a high degree of partnership and close co-operation.

In Carey Street

Carey Street in the City of London is the home of the bankruptcy court and 'being in Carey Street' has become a euphemism for being bankrupt.

In the limelight

Lime-lights were so called because lime was an essential component in the burning process that produced a vivid light used in theatres from the mid-1800s. A lime-light was used to cast a beam of bright light on the central character on stage thus excluding the other players. From this has developed the current expression where being 'in the limelight' describes being in the full glare of public attention.

In a nutshell

The phrase as we use it today means that something can be explained in a few words. Ironically, there are examples throughout history of extraordinary feats of handwriting in which the whole text of the Bible or some other celebrated work has been written in letters so small that the completed work could be folded and enclosed within the shell of a walnut.

In the pink

Used in this context 'pink' does not refer to the colour but to a point, as in 'pinking-shears' characterized by their blades with pointed edges. To be 'in the pink', or to put it more fully, 'in the pink of condition' is to be in the best of health, the peak of fitness. In *Romeo and Juliet* Shakespeare refers to 'the very pink of courtesy' and Oliver Goldsmith's most popular play *She Stoops to Conquer* contains a reference to 'the very pink of perfection'.

In the swim

Those 'in the swim' find themselves ideally placed to further their position in society. The phrase comes from fishing in which a shoal of fish is frequently referred to as a 'swim'. An angler who succeeds in casting his bait 'in the swim' is sure to have a good catch.

Iron rations

Emergency supplies, especially those issued to the armed forces, were often referred to as iron rations because many of them took the form of tinned food. Today the term is used to describe a variety of basic emergency rations, preserved in various ways, that can be consumed with the minimum of preparation.

Irons in the fire

Keeping 'too many irons in the fire' was a risky business in a number of occupations. In an old-fashioned laundry, keeping too many flat irons warming on a fire ran the risk of their over-heating and thus scorching the items being ironed. A blacksmith who had too many irons in the fire of his forge risked damaging the metal he was working with if any of that became too hot. From these and similar examples the phrase has developed as a warning against having too many projects in hand at the same time.

It's all grist to the mill

'Grist' is the name given by millers to the quantity of grain to be ground at any one time. So when everything is 'grist to the mill' it means that it will all be ground and therefore turned to advantage or profit.

Jerry-built

This expression came into use during the nineteenth century when a great demand for housing resulted in the erection of hastily constructed insubstantial buildings. The problem was particularly acute in ports like Liverpool which saw huge increases in population and it seems likely that 'jerry built' came into being as an adaptation of the nautical term 'jury-rig' or 'jury-mast'. These were temporary repairs rigged up in emergencies and only designed to be used until proper repairs could be made in port; 'jury' in this context takes its meaning from *jour*, the French word for 'day'. Unfortunately jerry-built houses gave the appearance of being more substantial and durable than they turned out to be.

Jot or tittle

A 'jot or tittle' is a tiny amount, in most instances the smallest amount possible, as in the expression 'I don't give a jot or tittle.' Both of them are the tiniest amounts in their respective contexts. 'Jot' is a corruption of the name of the smallest letter in the Greek alphabet, *iota*. 'Tittle' comes from the medieval Latin word *titulus* which is the dot placed above the *i*.

Jumping over the broomstick

Among the most informal marriage practices was one that involved the happy couple doing nothing other than jumping over a broomstick to cement their status as man and wife. This curious custom was largely observed by itinerant communities such as gypsies, tinkers and wandering labourers. So 'jumping over the broomstick' has come to describe a marriage that takes place quite informally without significant preparation or ceremony.

Junk

Although we use 'junk' today to describe almost anything that has served its purpose and is no longer wanted, it was first coined by early seafarers to describe old rope. The word 'junk' probably comes from the Latin word *juncus*, meaning a 'rush' from which early ropes were made.

Kangaroo court

A 'kangaroo court' is a self-appointed assembly with no legal status which sits in judgement on members of the same group who are deemed to have contravened its rules. The phrase has

106

been used disparagingly in the past of some trade union bodies which have passed 'judgement' on union members who have acted or spoken against the broad mass of opinion. The connection with the kangaroo may stem from the series of unfettered bounds the 'court' makes in reaching its judgement and 'kangaroo courts' were common among the early convict communities in Australia.

Keel-hauling

This phrase, used to describe a severe castigation, vividly captures a brutal form of punishment once meted out in the navy. Those sentenced to be keel-hauled were dragged by ropes from one side of a ship below the surface and under the keel until they emerged on the other side. In addition to almost being drowned, offenders suffered severe lacerations and it was not uncommon for death to follow a keel-hauling.

Keeping up with the Joneses

Anyone trying to maintain appearances or keep on the social level of their neighbours has been 'keeping up with the Joneses' since before the First World War. In 1913 a cartoon series began to be syndicated in newspapers throughout the USA based on the attempts by the artist, Arthur R. ('Pop') Momand, to keep up with his neighbours. It was he who invented the phrase.

Kicking the bucket

This euphemism for dying originated in the traditional practice of killing a pig for winter. The wooden frame from which the pig's carcass was suspended by the ankles is known in East Anglia as a 'bucket', from a French word *buquet* for a beam.

Kicking up a shindy

Shinty is a game resembling hockey, and 'shindy' may well be derived from it. 'Kicking up a shindy' means causing a commotion or a disturbance and may reflect the excitement from playing shinty.

Knuckling under

Today we reserve the word 'knuckle' to describe finger-joints, but in earlier times it had a wider meaning covering any bone that ended in a joint. In this context 'knuckling under' meant kneeling as a display of submission or admitting defeat. The phrase we use today carries the same meaning of giving in.

Kudos

'Kudos' is a straightforward example of one language borrowing a word directly from another language. In Greek *kudos* means 'renown' and the word shares the same meaning when it is used in English.

Land-lubber

A 'lubber' is a clumsy fellow in both Danish and English and a 'land-lubber' is a clumsy sailor, whose inexperience aboard ship soon shows him to be more used to life ashore.

Laughing stock

In the sixteenth century a 'stock' was an object of contemptuous treatment, perhaps by association with the wooden framework of the same name that was erected for the punishment of malefactors. 'Laughing stock' is a reinforcement of this, confirming someone as a butt of other people's jokes.

Laughing up one's sleeve

To call this a fashion statement is not being facetious. In the days when both men and women wore clothes with large loose sleeves it was possible to hide one's amusement by literally putting your face in your sleeve. The present-day expression takes its meaning of secret laughter and private derision from this practice of earlier times.

Left in the lurch

In its wider context 'left in the lurch' is an expression used to describe someone who has been abandoned in an awkward predicament. The term is derived from the game of cribbage and is used in the situation in which one player's pegs reach the end of the board before the other player's pegs have moved half-way round.

Lemon sole

Tasty as fish may be when lemon juice is added, a lemon sole has nothing to do with the citrus fruit. The 'lemon' part of its name is derived from the French word *limande*, which means a flat board – an apt description of this flatfish.

Letting the cat out of the bag

A secret is revealed if 'the cat is let out of the bag' and in the days when this originated that is precisely what happened. The cat would have been put in the bag by an unscrupulous market trader hoping to pass it off as a young sucking pig, similar to the one on open display at his stall. Unwitting buyers would pay for a pig in one of the sacks only to find later that they had bought a puppy or a cat instead. Those who had the good sense to check what they were buying would 'let the cat out of the bag' and reveal the trick that was being played on them.

[See: pig in a poke]

Lick into shape

In the Middle Ages there was once a widespread belief that bear cubs were born shapeless and had to be licked into the shape of bears by their mothers. Applied to human off-spring, it describes the process of rearing children to behave in an appropriate way and generally it means making things presentable.

Like a red rag to a bull

The image in this vivid phrase for anything liable to provoke an outburst of rage comes from the Spanish bullring where toreadors traditionally exhibit their skills using a red cape. Although it is the fluttering and movement of the cape that enrages the bull and not the colour, the phrase has become firmly rooted in the language.

Lily-livered

In the ancient world it was widely believed that cowards had less blood in their livers than their braver comrades. As a result of this, phrases such as 'lily-livered' came to be applied to anyone who showed signs of cowardice. In spite of a better understanding of human anatomy, the phrase has remained fixed in the language.

Lionize

Until the beginning of the last century the Tower of London acted as a royal zoo, where the lions were the main attraction for visitors. A celebrity fêted by a host or hostess could be said to be 'lionized', if he or she was put on similar 'display' before company in the hope that they would be suitably impressed by the 'catch'.

Living quarters

In the armed services living quarters are categorized in various ways, such as married quarters. Aboard ship the quarter-deck was the area reserved for officers and in the army the quartermaster included the allocation of accommodation among his other responsibilities. In all these cases 'quarter' is derived from the French verb *écarter*, 'to set apart'.

Lock, stock and barrel

The lock, the stock and the barrel are the three principal components of a gun. Brought together in this time-honoured expression, they mean the whole of anything as in an expression like, 'They bought everything, lock, stock and barrel.'

[See: going the whole hog; the whole caboodle]

Long chalk

This refers more accurately to a long line of chalk marks, such as those used to mark the score in a game. To be beaten or outdone by a 'long chalk' is to lose decisively.

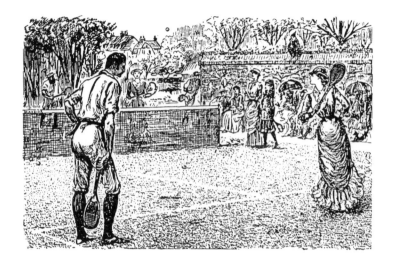

Love

In tennis and several other ball and racket games 'love' is the score meaning 'nil'. The explanation for this becomes clearer when we discover that 'love' in this context is a pun on the French word *l'oeuf*, meaning 'the egg', the shape represented by the zero of 'nil'.

[See: out for a duck]

Lukewarm

This is an example of a current word formed from two separate words of the same meaning. In Old English the word *hleow* meant 'warm' and this, combined with the more familiar word of the same sound and meaning, produced 'lukewarm' which we use today to describe temperatures that are tepid.

Mad as a hatter

A mercury-based chemical used in the manufacture of felt hats was thought to be responsible for creating tremulous conditions such as St Vitus Dance in those who were exposed to them for a prolonged period. The nature of their trade made hatters susceptible, though the phrase owes much of its popularity to Lewis Carroll who popularized it in *Alice in Wonderland*.

Mad as a March hare

Hares breed in March and this is the time of the year when they perform their energetic and athletic courtship displays. To anyone observing these, the hares appear to be behaving in a very peculiar way, which could be construed as a sign of 'madness'.

Make and mend

'Make and mend' times are now regarded as periods of time without any particular task allotted to them. In days gone by 'make and mend' applied to time given over in the Royal Navy each week for the repair of clothing and kit.

Make no bones about it

Saying or doing something without delay regardless of the consequences is to 'make no bones about it'. As a process of coming straight to the point, it takes its origins from dice, which were once referred to as bones. There is an expression in French which describes sliding the dice, a process that has been taken as softening something down. This is the precise opposite of the English expression, which has no interest in manipulating the dice to curry favour. Plain speaking is the order of the day when we 'make no bones' about something.

Making bricks without straw

In the *Book of Exodus* the Egyptians command the Israelites to make bricks without straw, a process which is doomed to failure, for without straw the bricks will crumble and break. Thus any attempt to do something without proper materials and preparation will meet a similar fate.

Man of straw

These days a 'man of straw' is a merely a front-man for an enterprise, one with no substance. The unusual term is originates from the equally insincere practice adopted by men who once frequented courts of law in the hope that they would be paid to appear as witnesses and swear to whatever was asked of them. To draw attention to themselves they carried a straw in their shoes.

Mealy-mouthed

'Smarmy' is a word that often springs to mind when someone is described as 'mealy-mouthed'. A German idiom of similar origins describes 'carrying meal in the mouth', as an image of someone who does not speak coherently or straightforwardly. 'Mealy-mouthed' is the English variant of this expression used by Martin Luther, among others.

Mentor

This is another word that has been adopted into English from the ancient world. We use 'mentor' to describe someone who acts as a wise counsellor and friend who guides us along an appropriate course of action. Homer's *Odyssey* is the setting in which the original Mentor comes into being as a friend of Odysseus. In Homer's epic poem, the goddess Minerva disguises herself as Mentor when she accompanies the hero's son, Telemachus, in his search for his father.

Merry

When 'merry' was first used in English it simply meant 'pleasing' and 'agreeable', as in the phrase Merrie England or the Christmas carol 'God rest you merry, gentlemen'. The more riotous meaning of mirthful jollity it carries now is a later development, though it is similar to an old Dutch word for 'mirth', *merchte*.

Minding your Ps and Qs

As a warning to watch how you behave it's possible that 'minding your Ps and Qs' originated in the genteel surroundings of the French court in the seventeenth century. There dancing instructors would caution their pupils to mind their *pieds* (feet) and *queues* (tails of their wigs) when they took to the floor. On such occasions dancers who bowed their heads too low when making formal bows risked losing their tall elaborate wigs which were liable to slip off their heads and cause considerable embarrassment. Nearer home, 'Ps and Qs' have also been linked to the practice of publicans who kept an account of how much beer their customers drank by marking pints under 'P' and quarts (two pints) under 'Q'. Customers were well advised to keep a check on their 'Ps and Qs' to avoid being overcharged when it came to the final reckoning.

Mob

The first 'mobs' in the current sense of the word were in ancient Roman, where they were referred to by the Latin expression *mobile vulgus* , the 'fickle crowd'. By the seventeenth century the opinions of the ordinary people were beginning to be widely voiced in England and the word *mobile* was soon shortened to the 'mob' we retain today.

Molly coddle

In the early nineteenth century a 'molly' was a slang expression for an effeminate man, or milksop. This, joined with 'coddle' meaning to pamper or spoil, produced the term that has passed down to us as a way of fussing over someone as one fusses over children or weaklings.

Moot point

In Anglo-Saxon times a 'moot' was a gathering of freemen who came together to decide a point of local government. The word passed into legal circles where it was applied to debates held among students in the Inns of Court. By the sixteenth century 'moot' was being used as an adjective meaning 'debatable' or 'arguable' which gave rise to the 'moot point' familiar to us now as a point open to debate and further discussion.

Mosey along

'Moseying along' and 'moseying around' are expressions that crossed the Atlantic from the United States during the nineteenth century. They both refer to an exploratory saunter, conducted without hurry, and both derive from a corruption of the Spanish *vamose*, meaning 'let's go'.

Mufti

In military circles 'mufti' denoted plain clothes worn off-duty, as opposed to uniform that was worn on-duty. The term probably arose among British troops serving in the Middle East where some army officers were accustomed to relaxing in dressing-gown, smoking cap and slippers. This outfit bore similarities to the stage costume adopted at the time to denote a Mohammedan priest or sage, referred to in Arabic as a *mufti*. This association moved from the theatre to the barracks where 'mufti' was adopted as a general expression for wearing civilian clothes.

Mumbo Jumbo

'Mumbo Jumbo' entered the English language in the writings of Mungo Park, the nineteenth-century explorer of the Niger region of West Africa. Park described Mumbo Jumbo as a fictitious god, who was impersonated by men of the tribes he encountered, in order to terrify their women-folk and keep them under their control. In time the frightening deity Mumbo Jumbo changed to 'mumbo jumbo' the incomprehensible nonsense in the form we use it today.

Nab

When somebody or something is 'nabbed' they are seized unexpectedly and without warning. Scandinavian words such as *nappa* have a similar meaning and share a common root with their counterpart in English. The English word 'kidnap' is even closer to these Nordic words.

Nagging

'Nagging' is another word with a Scandinavian ancestry. Both Norwegian and Swedish have the word *nagga* meaning 'to gnaw' or to 'irritate'. The description of persistent discomfort as a 'nagging pain' recalls this early meaning and the more common use of 'nagging' to describe relentless irritating scolding is a direct extension.

Nail drives out nail

It is quite common for a new nail to be used as a punch to drive an old nail out of a piece of timber. This process of expelling something, or someone, of long-standing with a new replacement has many resonances in life and the phrase has become a well-established proverb.

Namby-pamby

Ambrose Philips was a poet who died in 1749 and whose verse was ridiculed by more accomplished poets, like Alexander Pope, for what they regarded as its childish sentimentality. Pope was one of the poets who coined the name 'Namby-Pamby' on Ambrose Philips's name and the nickname has stuck in the language as an adjective describing anything weakly sentimental and insipid.

Nap

'Nap' is the shortened version of an Old English word *hnappian* meaning 'to take a short sleep'.

Natty

By the eighteenth century 'natty' was in common use to describe someone or something that was smartly neat – in fact 'natty' is probably a corruption of 'neat'. A century later 'natty' acquired its secondary meaning of 'clever' and 'deft'. So the word came to be used to describe someone who was 'nattily' dressed and also a 'natty' activity or function that was deft or neatly performed.

Navvy

The 'navvy' made his first appearance during the Industrial Revolution in the eighteenth century when gangs of labourers were engaged in the construction of earthworks for canals, and later railways, throughout the British Isles. In their early days the canals were called 'navigations' and the men who dug them were 'navigators'. This was soon abbreviated to 'navvy' and the word was adopted to describe anyone working on an excavation.

Neck and heels

This unusual way of conveying the idea of entirety occurs in expressions such as 'I threw him out neck and heels', meaning 'I threw him out wholeheartedly'. It may derive its meaning from a form of punishment in which a culprit's knees were pushed up to touch his chin so that he could be shoved into a small cage.

Nest-egg

Today a 'nest-egg' is a sum of money safely put away as a reserve. When the term was first recorded early in the seventeenth century it described a sum of money set aside as an encouragement to save further money. This earlier meaning is an allusion to the practice of placing an egg, even an artificial egg, in a hen's nest to encourage her to lay others.

Newfangled

The Old English word *fangol* means 'inclined to take' and combined with 'new' it gives us the word used to describe things whose sole appeal lies in the fact that they are new. At one time the people who were easily carried away by new ideas were described as 'newfangled'.

News

The fact that 'news' reaches us from all directions has led to the understandable, but false, belief that the word is derived from the initials of the four principal points of the compass: North, East,

West and South. In its earliest form in English 'news' was spelt 'newes', which dismisses the compass associations. In fact 'news' is simply the plural of 'new' and its meaning is similar to that of the French word *nouvelles*, meaning 'new things'. Although 'news' is plural, it is referred to these days as a singular noun, as in 'Today's news is good'. However, this is a fairly recent development. Only a century ago people were still referring to 'news' in the plural, turning the sentence above into 'Today's news are good'.

Nickname

Until the thirteenth century nicknames were often used instead of surnames. These were not nicknames in the sense that we know them today, that is to say, humorous or sometimes pejorative names. They were additional names that helped to identify those to whom they were given. In Old English they were referred to as *ekenames*, meaning 'also names'. In the singular *an ekename* became 'a nickname' when the *a* of *an* was shifted to the beginning of *ekename*. Changes such as this were not uncommon as the language developed. In time *eke* became 'nick' and the alteration in the spelling was complete.

Nincompoop

This expressive word combines a number of elements that refer to a simpleton. 'Ninny' came into being as a pet-form of the name Innocent, with an *n* added as a prefix, just as Neddy is a pet-form of Eddy with an *n* at the beginning. 'Poop' is related to the Dutch word *poep* which means 'a fool'. Brought together by the seventeenth century they aptly describe a gullible simpleton.

Nine days' wonder

The origin of this phrase, commonly used to describe something that causes a short-lived sensation before being quickly forgotten, may lie in the proverb 'A wonder last nine days and then the puppy's eyes are open'. The reference here is to the fact that puppies are born blind and cannot see until they are nine days old, just as people can be temporarily 'blinded' by some 'wonder' until they finally 'see' through it and the 'wonder' ceases to interest them.

Nineteen to the dozen

These days 'nineteen to the dozen' is generally used to describe someone who cannot stop talking. However, the sense of ceaseless activity came into being from the early days of steam engines, notably those used to power pumps in mines. A steam engine going 'nineteen to the dozen' was pumping 19,000 gallons of water for every twelve bushels of coal it burned. Far from describing a somewhat wasteful activity, which may be the case today, it was originally a measure of efficiency.

No great shakes

A 'shake' of the dice is another way of describing a throw of the dice and a shake or throw that does not add up to very much is self-evidently not a great shake. 'No great shakes' reflects this in its meaning of being unremarkable and not particularly impressive.

Nonplussed

When someone is described as being 'nonplussed' he or she is rendered speechless or unable to act by whatever has just been said or has passed. In this state nothing more can be added to what they have already said or done. 'Nonplussed' has its origins in two Latin words *non plus* which mean 'not more' or 'no further'.

Not worth a rush

In medieval times rushes were important domestic commodities. They were strewn on floors and important visitors were treated to clean, freshly strewn rushes. Rushes were also bound in bundles to be as used as torches. So anything or anyone considered to be 'not worth a rush' was of very little importance, in other words they were worthless.

Not worth his salt

In ancient Rome soldiers and workers employed by the state received part of their wages in salt. The Latin word for 'salt' is *salarium*, from which we get the word 'salary'. This is recalled in the expression 'not worth his salt', meaning that whoever was being paid was not working well enough to be worth his salary.

Nous

In English 'nous' is one of several common words for 'intelligence' and 'understanding'. It has the same associations with the mind and intellect in Greek from which it was incorporated directly into English.

OK

Meaning 'all right', 'all correct', OK came into widespread use in the USA during the first half of the nineteenth century. Its similarity with words of the same meaning in native American Indian languages and several languages spoken by slaves brought from West Africa must have helped its rise in popular usage, but OK got its greatest boost as a political slogan. In this context OK was an abbreviation for 'Old Kinderhook', the nickname given to the Democratic politician Martin Van Buren. Kinderhook was his birthplace in New York state. When he ran for the presidential election in 1840, Democrats all over the country were encouraged to voice their support for Old Kinderhook, or OK, because in the eyes of his supporters he was 'orl korrect' (all correct). So the politician and his policies became a rallying cry as the country went to the polls. Even though OK failed to win the election, the term associated with him had caught on and soon made its way round the rest of the English-speaking world.

On the cards

For an event to be 'on the cards' there is a strong likelihood that it will happen. This sense of optimism may have been derived from the use of cards to tell fortunes, or from a likely win among the runners on a racing programme or 'card'.

On the nod

In an auction room bids can be accepted by the auctioneer on the nodding of the bidder's head. This is taken as a willingness to buy, although the actual payment only takes place after the auction is over. From this specific reference 'on the nod' has developed into a wider meaning of buying on credit, when payment is deferred until after the actual time of purchase.

On tenterhooks

The origins of this vivid expression have become obscured with time but when it was coined it was a well-drawn metaphor for a state of painful suspense, which it still means today. A 'tenter' is a wooden frame used to stretch freshly-woven cloth and the 'tenterhooks' are the hooks on the frame that secure the cloth as it is being stretched.

On your beam ends

To be 'on one's beam ends' is to be in serious trouble, much as a wooden ship was considered to be in a desperate predicament when the wind and sea forced it to heel right over on its side. Such ships had large wooden beams running across the framework from side to side. They supported the decks and held the sides together. To be on the 'beam ends' then, was to be heeling over at an alarming angle.

Out for a duck

A batsman who is out without scoring is said to be 'out for a duck'. The phrase was originally 'a duck's egg' which makes more sense since the shape of the duck's egg resembles the 0 of the score. In North America the similar term for no score is goose-egg.

[See: love]

Out-of-sorts

When someone is described as being 'out-of-sorts' he or she is not in the best of health and generally in low spirits. When cards are in the wrong order they are also described as being 'out of sorts'. The expression is also used in the printing industry where a printer is 'out of sorts' if he is short of some of the letters or characters needed in his case.

Painting the king's picture

Among criminals 'painting the king's picture' is a euphemism for forging money. In days gone by this applied particularly to coins, since most coins carried the monarch's head on one side.

Palming off

Today 'palming off' something implies that a purchaser has been persuaded to buy it in the mistaken belief that it is of greater value than it actually is. In other words it is a euphemism for an act of fraud. When the phrase was first coined it conveyed a sense of illusion rather than criminal deceit. Conjurors perfected the art of 'palming off' things to create the illusion of their disappearance in one place and reappearance in another, while all the time they are concealed in the palm of the conjuror's hand.

Pandemonium

In his epic poem *Paradise Lost* John Milton named the principal city in Hell, Pandemonium, which means 'all the devils' in Greek. With residents such as these it isn't surprising that Milton's city became synonymous with the wild, unrestrained uproar with which we associate a 'pandemonium' now.

Pan out

When something 'pans out' it turns out satisfactorily, just as a prospector hopes his search for gold will be rewarded as he swirls gravel in the water of a shallow pan where any gold present will be separated from the gravel. The expression is in fact derived from the panning system of gold prospecting.

Paraphernalia

At one time 'paraphernalia' had a special meaning for married women, for it was the legal term that covered their personal possessions which they could legitimately claim as their own, since they were not part of the dowry paid to their husbands at the time they were married. The word is formed from two Greek words *para* (beside) and *pherne* (dowry). These days 'paraphernalia' covers a wide range of personal possessions or apparatus and no longer applies exclusively to married women.

Passing the buck

'Passing the buck' today means evading responsibility or shifting the blame on to someone else. This was not always the case. When the expression was first used it was little more than a way of reminding poker players whose turn it was to be dealer of the next hand. In this case the reminder was a 'buck', possibly a piece of buck-shot, which was passed round the table from one dealer to the next.

Paying on the nail

Payment 'on the nail' has always been payment made immediately on the receipt of goods (or services) without difficulty or delay. As a turn of phrase and a trading practice it dates from the medieval market-place where deals were frequently contracted in public in the presence of witnesses. These transactions took place at a 'nail', a flat-topped pillar on which goods were displayed by the seller and where payment was placed by the buyer as soon as he or she was satisfied with what was on offer.

Paying through the nose

Various theories are put forward to explain the origin of this graphic expression for anyone forced to pay more for something than it is really worth. One explanation links it with a form of early taxation imposed by Danish invaders, who punished those who refused to pay by slitting their noses. Another draws an analogy between a bleeding nose and someone who is 'bled' by being obliged to pay an excessive price.

L. JOHNSON & CO.

Pecking order

The hierarchy that once existed among farmyard hens has now transferred to human society where unofficial orders of precedence and superiority are created in all walks of life. Hens sort themselves into a ranking, at the top of which one hen rules supreme and is able to peck all the others without retaliation, while at the bottom is a wretched bird that is pecked by all the others without being able to peck back. Between these two extremes the other hens are ranked in pecking order. The same is said to apply, metaphorically, to humans.

Pedigree

When a genealogist drew up a family tree, the ancestral lines of descent were marked by an arrow-like symbol. To some this looked like the foot of a crane, which in Old French was rendered *pie de gru*. In time the spelling was altered and the word was absorbed into the English language where it came to refer to the family tree in general.

Peg away

The game of cribbage, in which players build up their score by moving pegs around the board, gives rise to this expression. 'Pegging away' implies steady, persistent application to a task, often in the face of set-backs.

Peppercorn rent

Nominal rents of negligible value are sometimes paid by tenants who are allowed to occupy premises owned by others almost free of charge. These are referred to as 'peppercorn rents' since a peppercorn, though of very little value, still represents a financial exchange between tenant and landlord. This is important as it confirms the owner's ultimate rights to the property.

Peter out

In the Californian goldfields of the mid-nineteenth century the explosive used to open up seams was known as 'peter' from the saltpetre it contained. When a seam was fully exploited and no further work could take place the miners described it as having 'petered out' and the phrase has developed as an expression meaning 'to cease gradually'.

Picnic

The English word 'picnic' was developed from a similar sounding French word *piquenique*, which came into being towards the end of the seventeenth century as a name for a social get-together in which all of those attending contributed a share of the food. Half-a-century later the 'picnic' had moved outdoors and had acquired the meaning it retains to this day of an outdoor party and meal.

Pidgin English

Although this trading language is sometimes spelt 'pigeon English', 'pidgin' is the correct form, for the word approximates to a Chinese speaker's pronunciation of the English word 'business'. Pidgin English developed as an effective means of communication along the coast of China after English ships began trading there from the seventeenth century onwards. Although an artificial language, it proved to be a successful means of conducting business between speakers of English and Chinese, incorporating as it does elements from both. Pidgin Englishes have developed for similar reasons in other parts of the world with equal success. In one instance they have found their way back to the UK where the expression 'That's my pidgin (pigeon)' means 'That's my business'.

[See: chop-chop]

Pig in a poke

As an unseen bargain a 'pig in a poke' is a risky purchase. In the days when sucking pigs were sold live at markets, it was not uncommon for unscrupulous traders to place one pig on display and offer others for sale tied up in bags. Unless the purchaser looked inside the bag to ensure he or she was really buying a pig, they could well hand over their money only to discover later that they had actually bought a puppy or a cat. So much for the 'pig', what about the 'poke'? This is actually the English version of the French word for a 'bag', *poche*. So a 'pig in a poke' was offered for sale as a 'pig in a bag', but it was up to the buyer to make sure what the bag contained.

[See: letting the cat out of the bag]

Pig and whistle

This unlikely pairing which is used as the name for many English public houses is in all likelihood the corrupt spelling of two Old English words *piggin* and *wassail*. The first of these was an earthenware container from which drinkers filled their own mugs and *wassail* was a traditional greeting used when drink was offered to a guest or when a toast was drunk to his health. Put together the *piggin* and *wassail* seem an ideal combination for a public house; it's only the changes in spelling that have obscured their origins and given pub sign-painter's endless scope for their creative powers.

Pinning your heart on your sleeve

The world of the Middle Ages is recalled in this chivalrous reference to knights who went into a tournament wearing a token of their ladies'. In modern times those who make their affections apparent for all the world to see are said to have 'pinned their hearts on their sleeves'.

Pitched battle

A 'pitched battle' is a battle that takes place on a site previously selected or 'pitched' before fighting begins. As such it is a planned battle, as opposed to a skirmish or chance encounter between opposing armies.

Plain as a pikestaff

Although pikestaffs measuring sixteen feet in length are not commonly seen today, they were familiar and unmistakable objects in the sixteenth century when the pikestaff was the principal weapon of the foot soldiers known as pikemen. In spite of this historical lapse, anything described as being 'as plain as a pikestaff' is still as blindingly obvious today as it would have been four hundred years ago.

Playing fast and loose

There is an air of trickery and deceit in 'playing fast and loose', which implies saying one thing and doing another. The expression dates from an old fairground trick at which unsuspecting victims were persuaded to bet they could pin a folded belt to a board by passing a skewer through the loop. The trickster then folded the belt in such a way that the feat was almost impossible and invariably when the belt was pulled away it was shown not to be fast, but loose, so the victim lost his bet.

Post haste

By the sixteenth century the fastest means of travel was to go 'post haste'. Rather than riding the whole distance on one's own horse which was likely to tire as the journey progressed, travelling post haste consisted of riding a fresh mount from one fixed location to another, where another fresh horse could be obtained. This was how the mail was conveyed around the country and 'post haste' came to mean 'with the greatest speed'.

Pot-boiler

'Pot-boilers' are frequently works produced by artists and writers who undertake them without regard to any intrinsic literary or artistic merit. 'Pot-boilers' are produced with the sole purpose of earning money to keep the domestic 'pot' boiling, in other words to provide the basic necessities of life and pay the bills.

Pot luck

Dining off the contents of the family cooking pot which was kept hot over the fire and into which everything that 'had gone to pot' was put, was always something of a lottery. Taking 'pot luck' now is taking a chance, in the same way that those sitting down to eat what was in the pot had no idea what to expect.

[See: gone to pot]

Pouring oil on troubled waters

Seafarers have known for centuries that oil poured onto the surface of the sea will reduce the violence of the waves. The term acquired its metaphorical use in the middle of the nineteenth century when it was first used to describe the use of calming words and behaviour to restore harmony after an argument or an outburst of anger.

Punch

When British settlers began to explore the Indian sub-continent for the first time during the second half of the seventeenth century one of the most popular discoveries was the Indian drink named *punch*. This was a mixture of five ingredients: water, spirit, sugar, spice, and a sharp fruit juice such as lemon. In Hindi *punch* is simply the number 'five', for the five ingredients, and the name of the drink has been adopted directly into English and many other European languages.

Pundit

'Pundit' is another word brought back from India where a *pandit* is a Hindu scholar, well versed in Sanskrit, the law and ancient scriptures. In English the word has been adopted with a slightly modified spelling and applies to an 'expert' in a particular field of scholarship.

Putting the kibosh on

To 'put the kibosh on' something is to put an end to it for once and for all. Various origins have been suggested. One traces a link with a Yiddish word *kabas*, meaning 'to suppress'. Another looks to a hunting term used in Scotland, *caboche*, which is the process of cutting off a deer's head close behind the horns. There is also an Irish expression *cie bais*, in which the second word is pronounced 'bosh'. This is translated as 'cap of death'. Whichever explanation is chosen, they all have a sense of finality.

Putting on the lugs

'Lug', the old word for the 'ear' also meant 'to put on airs'. So anyone 'putting on the lugs' is giving themselves airs and acting in a conceited way.

Putting salt on his tail

The belief that putting salt on a bird's tail enabled one to catch it has given rise to this expression for apprehending someone.

Quack

Although trained doctors are sometimes unfairly described as 'quacks' by disgruntled patients, the original 'quacks' were wandering charlatans who purported to sell 'wonder-drugs' with remarkable healing properties. The present-day 'quack' is an abbreviated form of 'quacksalver', which is closely associated with a Dutch word *kwakzalver*. He was a rogue who boasted of the efficacy of his cures ('salves') like a quacking duck.

Quibble

As a fine point of detail, often used as a means of evading a direct question or obscuring what the speaker would rather not admit, a 'quibble' owes its existence to legal documentation. The word has been recorded in English since the seventeenth century when it appears to have developed as a play on words that made fun of the subtle distinctions and hair-splitting definitions that characterized so many legal documents. The Latin word *quibus* meaning 'to whom' occurred so frequently in legal documentation that it came to symbolize legal subtleties. 'Quibble' is a pun on *quibus*, meaning a small evasive detail.

Quiz

'Quiz' is a prime example of an invented word. According to the story surrounding it, 'quiz' was devised in 1780 by a Dublin theatre manager named Daly. He wagered that he could introduce a new word with no meaning into the English language in just twenty-four hours. Daly's wager was accepted and all around the city the four letters q, u, i, z were chalked up on walls and doors. Daly won his bet as 'quiz' became the centre of attention and everyone tried to find out what it meant. 'Quiz' has carried this sense of enquiry ever since and today it is the name given to many sorts of competitive tests, frequently comprising general knowledge questions.

Rack and ruin

Like many similar English phrases 'rack and ruin' trips off the tongue as a descriptive turn of phrase. In this instance it describes a state of total decay and destruction, in which 'rack' is an alternative spelling of 'wrack' which itself is a variant of the more familiar noun 'wreck'.

Raining cats and dogs

According to Norse mythology the cat was closely associated with the weather; in fact witches were believed to disguise themselves as cats when they rode on storm clouds. Dogs too had connections with clouds through their status as attendants of Odin, the god of storms. Together they represented torrential rain and fierce wind that characterized the weather when it 'rained cats and dogs'.

Raising the wind

Just as a sailing ship cannot make headway without wind to fill the sails and drive her forward, so many business enterprises cannot proceed without borrowed capital. In this context 'wind' is a euphemism for money and 'raising the wind' means 'raising money'.

Ransack

The word we use today to describe the searching of premises, often with an eye to robbery or plunder, is a modern version of an Old Norse word *rannsaka*. This meant 'to search for stolen goods' and is formed from the word for a 'house', *rann*, and *saka*, which is derived from the Norse verb for 'to seek'. So, where the original word meant to search for goods that had been stolen, the meaning has shifted to a search for goods that might be stolen.

Red-letter day

'Red-letter days' are days to be looked forward to and remembered with special pleasure. In bygone days, saints' days and important Christian feast days were printed in red ink in the church calendar to distinguish them from all the other days in the church year which were printed in black.

Red herring

We only use part of the original expression today, which makes its meaning more difficult to deduce at first glance. In its complete form the expression is 'drawing a red herring across the path'. The herring in question was dried and smoked, much like a present-day kipper. Like a kipper it had a distinctive and powerful aroma and it was popularly believed that if a red herring was drawn across the path taken by a fox, it would destroy its scent and so divert the pursuing hounds from their quarry. In our abbreviated usage, a 'red herring' has come to symbolize any device that is used to divert attention from the main issue under consideration or investigation.

Right as a trivet

Anything that is 'right as a trivet' is in the best possible state, because a trivet is a three-legged stand which can only stand in an upright position. Therefore to be 'right as a trivet' is to be quite right about something.

Right-hand man

As the senior assistant a 'right-hand man' was accorded pride of place over other servants and traditionally this was on his master's right-hand side. In this position he was better placed to fend off attack with the use of his sword. And occupying a position of such importance he was as indispensable to his master as his own right hand.

Ringing the changes

In traditional English bell-ringing, changes are rung using all the combinations of a set of bells. This is extended into everyday speech as an allusion to re-using the same limited resources in a variety of inventive ways.

Ringing up the curtain

At one time a bell was rung to signal the raising of the curtain in a theatre. From this the phrase has been adopted to describe inaugurating any new undertaking.

Robbing Peter to pay Paul

Peter and Paul have been seen as contrasting figures since early Christian times and there are no specific references to any particular Peter or Paul in this widely used saying. The meaning is plain: there is no point in paying off one debt if doing so means incurring another.

Run amok

This is a word borrowed from Malaysia, just as *berserk* was borrowed from Norway. They share a similar meaning. 'To run amok', or 'To go berserk' means to be seized by a sudden violent, destructive frenzy.

Running the gamut

'Running the gamut' is a process in which one covers the full range of whatever is the focus of attention. We frequently refer to 'running the gamut of emotions', in which one experiences either end of the emotional 'scale'. 'Gamut' in fact has a close association with music. The word is formed from two of the names given to notes in the original musical scale as devised in the ninth century by Guido d'Arezzo. *Gamma*, the third letter of the Greek alphabet, was the name given to the lowest note. *Ut* was the name of the first note in the scale used in singing – today we use 'doh'. So *gamma* and *ut* came together as *gamut* to describe the whole scale and, by extension, a full range in general.

Running the gauntlet

Those who 'run the gauntlet' are assailed or criticized on all sides. When the expression was first used in the seventeenth century it took the form of 'running the gantlope', *gantlope* being a word formed from two Swedish words *gata* meaning a 'passage' and *lopp* a 'course'. 'Running the gauntlet' was initially a form of punishment used in the Swedish armed forces. Two lines of men were drawn up facing each other and each man was equipped with a truncheon or rope's end with which he had to beat the man being punished, who was made to run down the narrow passage between them. In time *gantlope* changed its spelling and adopted the form of 'gauntlet', which of course is a type of glove.

Sent to Coventry

Being 'sent to Coventry' amounts to becoming a social outcast. Those who are 'sent to Coventry' are ignored by other people who refuse to speak to them or to acknowledge their presence. During the Civil War the city of Coventry was a strong outpost of Parliamentary support and Royalist prisoners captured in the Midlands were frequently sent to Coventry where the local population would have nothing to do with them.

Setting the Thames on fire

This phrase is usually used in the negative, as in 'He'll never set the Thames on fire', meaning 'He'll never make much of a mark in life'. It has been in use since the eighteenth century, but the principal rivers of other countries have been used in a similar context for longer and they all share a common meaning.

Shanks's pony

When we remember that the 'shank' is the part of our leg between the ankle and the knee, the meaning of this expression becomes clear. To go on 'Shank's pony' of course means to go by foot.

Shilly shally

To 'shilly shally' is to act undecidedly, to vacillate. The phrase is a variation of 'Shall I, shall I?' and in the seventeenth century took the form of 'to go shill I, shall I'.

Short shrift

'Shrift' is the penance imposed after confession and 'short shrift' was the brief period of a few minutes in which a condemned criminal was allowed to make confession before he or she was executed. To give 'short shrift' to something means to make short work of it, to get it over and done with quickly.

Showing the white feather

A symbol of cowardice, the white feather took its chilling association from cockfighting. No fighting-cock with even a single white feather in its plumage could be considered pure-bred and if not pure-bred it was deemed to lack the courage and fighting spirit of a true fighting-cock. During the First World War it was not uncommon for civilian men to be presented with white feathers by women who saw their lack of uniform as a sign of cowardice. To be shown or given a white feather, then, is to be branded a coward.

Sitting above the salt

In days gone by noble families were accustomed to placing large silver salt cellars in the middle of their dining tables.

Distinguished members of the family and guests sat between the salt cellar and the head of the family. Those of lesser status sat further down the table, 'below the salt'. As a result 'sitting above the salt' means occupying a favoured place.

Sour grapes

The temptation to disparage anything beyond one's reach is deeply-rooted in human nature. Aesop knew all about this failing when he wrote his popular fable about the fox who tried unsuccessfully to reach a bunch of grapes that took his fancy. When he realized that they were unattainable he abandoned his efforts claiming that the grapes were sour anyway.

Sowing wild oats

In agricultural terms wild oats produce an undesirable unregulated crop in contrast to carefully cultivated grain. Too many oats in a horse's diet tend to make it friskier than usual. Both ideas are present in the popular expression 'sowing wild oats' when it is applied to youthful excesses (usually among young men) before they settle down to a steady existence in which they make the most of their adult lives.

Speaking by the card

In this context the card referred to is not a playing card, but the card of a ship's compass. 'Speaking by the card' is being careful with one's words, though speaking with as much anticipation of being in the right as the compass has in indicating the true direction of north and the correct course the ship is following.

Spick and span

The original version of this phrase was 'spick and span new' and like many others in this collection it came from the world of ships and shipping in which a *spic* was a nail or spike used in ship-building and a *span* was a chip of wood. New ships that had come straight from the shipyard contained shiny new nails and tell-tale wood chips left from the carpenters' work. Since those days the meaning has altered somewhat. The association with newness has been replaced with a broader sense of being neat, tidy and well-presented.

Spiking his guns

The earliest types of cannon were simple muzzle-loaded weapons which were 'fired' by igniting a charge of powder through a small touch-hole. If a spike was hammered into the touch-hole, the charge could not be ignited and consequently the cannon was put out of action. This simple act of military sabotage has been adopted as a general term for foiling an opponent's plans.

Stemming the flow

As will be apparent by now, many English words have their roots in words from old Nordic languages. This is an example of a Norse word that has been taken directly into English and retains most of its original spelling and all its original meaning. When we speak of 'stemming the flow' of blood from a cut or water from a burst pipe, we are using the old Norse word *stemma* which means 'to stop', 'to dam up' a water-course.

Straight from the horse's mouth

One way of establishing the age of a horse is to examine its front teeth. In the past this was accepted by many people as being the most accurate method of discovering the animal's age and 'straight from the horse's mouth' has become synonymous with the highest recognized authority on any subject.

[See: don't look a gift horse in the mouth]

Stuck up

Anyone who gives themselves superior airs is likely to be described as 'stuck up', a phrase which recalls the attitude adopted by a peacock which sticks up its train of feathers allegedly to show its importance and superiority over its fellows.

Stump up

'Stumpy' was nineteenth century slang for money, from which we get this expression for paying what is due and paying it right away.

Swinging the lead

Aboard ship it used to be the task of the leadsman to find the depth of water in which his ship was sailing by casting a lead weight attached to a measuring line ahead of the vessel and noting how much line disappeared below the surface. Lazy leadsmen merely went through the motions by swinging the lead and this, like many nautical expressions, has come ashore as a term to describe shirking any activity by making up a plausible excuse or feigning illness.

Taken aback

To be truly 'taken aback', we are surprised, astounded for a moment by something wholly unexpected, just as a sailing ship is when caught by a powerful gust of head-wind. The term 'aback' comes from the era of square-rigged ships and describes what happens when square-rigged sails are forced back against their masts and rigging by a sudden gust, checking the ship's forward motion for a moment.

Taking down a peg

There was once a strict hierarchy at sea displayed by the position of ship's colours after they had been raised. The greatest honour was conferred by flags flown at the top of the mast. The flags, and therefore the degree of honour they bestowed, could be lowered by pegs. To be 'taken down a peg' was to receive a reduction in the honour shown to you. This nautical practice has developed a metaphorical use for taking the conceit from a boastful or 'stuck-up' person.

Taking the gilt off the gingerbread

At one time gingerbread cakes were sold with a thin layer of gilt on the top. Sometimes this was genuine gold leaf, though in most cases it was imitation for obvious reasons. Whichever material was used it gave the gingerbread a rich, lustrous, golden appearance in marked contrast to the dark coloured cake that lay beneath. Once the gilt had been removed, the cake could be seen for what it really was. From this has grown the current expression 'to take the gilt off the gingerbread' which means to show something in its true light as worth far less than it initially appeared to be. As an extension it is used to describe the process of generally destroying an illusion.

Taking a rain-check

Here is a piece of baseball terminology that has been absorbed into the language at a general level and has now become well-established even in parts of the world where baseball is not part of the sporting heritage. A 'rain-check' for a baseball game is a ticket that entitles the holder to watch another game if the one for which the ticket was bought is rained off. With this in mind, the expression has acquired a wider meaning and now refers to a wish to accept an invitation at a later date. In refusing the invitation, the reply is frequently 'I'll take a rain-check on it', meaning 'I'd like to come another time'.

Taking umbrage

'Umbrage' is the old French word for 'shade' and 'shadow' and when we take umbrage we feel resentful at being overshadowed, or slighted, by someone else.

Tarmac

'Tarmac', the smooth surface treatment commonly laid on many roads, is a development of the road-making system devised in the 1820s by the Scottish engineer John Loudon McAdam. His system used crushed stone bound with gravel to produce a raised road surface that drained effectively. The use of a layer of tar to bind the surface material was a later development that gave rise to 'tarmacadam' and ultimately 'tarmac'.

Tarred with the same brush

At one time shepherds would treat cuts and other lesions on a sheep's skin with a brush dipped in tar. Several sheep would be treated at a time, if not the whole flock, and when the shepherd was finished they had all been 'tarred with the same brush'. In its wider meaning, the expression has a critical tone, implying that the group of people referred to all share the same faults.

Tea-caddy

Although a 'tea-caddy' is the English name for a tea container, the 'caddy' part is derived from a word in the Malay language for a quantity of tea. This was called a *kati* and it was a measurement of slightly more than an English pound that was widely used throughout south-east Asia.

Thinking cap

The metaphorical process of putting on your 'thinking cap' before giving the answer to a difficult problem recalls the placing of the cap on a judge's head when he passed sentence. This was later restricted to the passing of the death sentence alone.

Three sheets in the wind

In naval terminology a 'sheet in the wind' is a rope used to secure a sail that is allowed to hang free, leaving the sail to flap inefficiently instead of catching the breeze. The expression is also applied to a sailor who has had too much to drink. So, to be 'three sheets in the wind' is to have drunk way too much.

To boot

To gain anything 'to boot' is to obtain it in addition to what one was expecting, to gain it into the bargain. In this context 'boot' has no connection with footwear. It comes instead from an early English word *bot* which means 'profit', 'advantage'.

Topsy-turvy

Despite is its widespread use since the sixteenth century the precise origin of 'topsy-turvy' has never been fully identified. The meaning of the phrase, that things are 'upside down' has not altered and it is probable that *turvy* is derived from the Old English word *tirve*, meaning 'turn over'. Similarly, *topsy* may be a variation of 'top so'. Put together, 'top so turn over' conveys the idea of something being turned upside down.

Two strings to your bow

Wise archers always carried a spare bow-string for use in emergencies. This precaution ensured that they were never without a second means of killing their prey or defending themselves. Having 'two strings to your bow' therefore implies the careful preparation of an alternative means of achieving what you set out to do.

Turning the corner

Having got over the worst of any setback one can be said to have 'turned the corner'. The corner from which the expression originates is a geographical 'corner', in fact there are two: The Cape of Good Hope at the southern tip of Africa and Cape Horn at the southern tip of South America. In both cases ships that had sailed round the cape and were now setting sail for the rest of their voyage were said to have 'turned the corner'.

Turning the peats

In those areas of northern England where peat was traditionally burnt as a domestic fuel, a block of peat that was red-hot on one side was turned in the grate to provide warmth while the other side was turned to the fire to heat up. This gave rise to the use of 'turning the peats' as a euphemism for changing the subject.

Umpteen

'Umpteen' is a very large, though unspecified number, which is of comparatively recent origin, dating from the First World War when it was coined by army signallers. 'Umpty' was signallers' slang for a 'dash' in Morse Code, so a great many dashes became 'umpteen', borrowing '-teen' from the 'tens', such as: fourteen, fifteen, sixteen, seventeen and so on.

Up to the mark

To be 'up to the mark' something or someone needs to have achieved a recognized standard in the eyes of those whose opinion counts for something. In this case the 'mark' was originally the hallmark stamped on articles of gold and silver by the assay offices. Goods that satisfied quality guidelines received the hallmark as proof of their authenticity. Those that were rejected were deemed not to be 'up to the mark'.

Upset the apple cart

Two centuries ago 'Apple cart' was wrestlers slang for the body. So 'to upset the apple cart' meant to fell an adversary and thereby throw into confusion his plan of action.

Use your loaf

In rhyming slang a 'loaf of bread' means a 'head'. This is usually shortened to 'loaf' and telling someone 'use your loaf' means 'use your head', or 'use your brains'.

Walk your chalk

This is a phrase that applies to tenants and householders alike. At one time a tenant could be given notice to quit by the landlord chalking the door of his home. In the same way royal officials could commandeer houses for the royal retinue by marking them with chalk and sending the occupants on their way. In both cases the phrase originally came into being as 'Walk, you're chalked', but over time the punctuation was lost and the later version became the norm.

Wet blanket

A blanket soaked in water literally has a dampening effect, putting out fire and reducing heat. The same effect can be given to a particular enterprise by someone who casts doubt on it or expresses discouragement, making them a 'wet blanket'.

What the Dickens

The novelist Charles Dickens can rest easy in his grave, for this expression predates him by several centuries. The phrase means 'What the devil' and 'Dickens' probably derives from 'Old Nick' and other names for the Devil.

Whipper-snapper

A 'whipper-snapper' is an inexperienced and frequently precocious young person who is probably so called after a 'whipster', literally 'a cracker of whips' who was portrayed as a lively, mischievous individual.

Whistling for it

One thing you can be sure of these days is that if someone says 'You can whistle for it', there is very little chance that you will get what you hope for. This sarcastic tone was not always present. In the days of sailing ships it was popularly believed among sailors that a breeze could literally be 'whistled up' if a ship was becalmed. When something was whistled for then, it was with hope and a strong sense of expectation.

The whole caboodle

Meaning 'the whole lot', 'absolutely everything', 'the whole caboodle' has an interesting international ancestry. 'Caboodle' probably comes from the Dutch word *boedel*, meaning 'possession', 'property', 'household goods'. The word has been in common use among New England longshoremen from the days of the first settlers in the New World. The American expression 'the whole kit and caboodle' has a similar meaning.

[See: lock, stock and barrel; going the whole hog]

Wide berth

In the language of seamanship a ship's berth is the place where the vessel is anchored or tied up. Ships lying at anchor could move in any direction around the anchor point and it was important that space was left for them to swing freely, without colliding with other vessels moored too close. To give a 'wide berth', is to keep at a safe distance from a person or an object.

Winning hands down

Here is an expression drawn from the world of racing where jockeys, whose mounts are so far ahead of the rest of field that they need no further urging towards the finish, drop their hands and let their horses run home at their own pace. From this easy victory comes the expression that is now applied to any success that is achieved comfortably and without any need to force the pace.

Winning plaudits

We tend to use 'plaudit' in a metaphorical sense meaning approbation and approval and the word has always had this meaning of seeking popular favour. Our English word is simply a corrupt form of the Latin word *plaudite*, meaning 'Applaud ye!'. This was the request made by Roman actors who used to walk to the edge of the stage to ask their audiences to applaud them.

With flying colours

The image conveyed by the expression 'with flying colours' is one of total, unequivocal, success, recalling as it does a fleet returning from a victorious action still flying its colours at the mastheads.

Without batting an eyelid

The 'batting' referred to in this common expression has nothing to do with striking anything. As a description of reacting to something without showing surprise, the 'batting' is best pictured as 'blinking'. The word is actually taken from an obsolete English word *bate*, meaning 'to beat the wings' or 'to flutter'.

Working up to the collar

In the days when horses supplied the brunt of drawing power on the land and on the roads, horses that pulled with their collars drawn up to their shoulders were clearly making a great effort. In contrast horses that had their collars hanging loosely round their necks could not be working anything like as hard. 'Working up to the collar' therefore means working with real effort, avoiding any attempt to take things easy.